THE GREAT AMERICAN STICKUP

ALSO BY ROBERT SCHEER

The Pornography of Power: How Defense Hawks Hijacked 9/11 and Weakened America

Playing President: My Close Encounters with Nixon, Carter, Bush I, Reagan, and Clinton—and How They Did Not Prepare Me for George W. Bush

The Five Biggest Lies Bush Told Us About Iraq (with coauthors Christopher Scheer and Lakshmi Chaudhry)

Thinking Tuna Fish, Talking Death: Essays on the Pornography of Power

With Enough Shovels: Reagan, Bush and Nuclear War

America After Nixon: The Age of the Multinationals

Cuba: Tragedy in Our Hemisphere (with coauthor Maurice Zeitlin)

How the United States Got Involved in Vietnam

EDITED BY ROBERT SCHEER

The Cosmetic Surgery Revolution

Eldridge Cleaver: Post-Prison Writings and Speeches by the Author of "Soul on Ice"

The Diary of Che Guevara

THE
GREAT AMERICAN
STICKUP

HOW REAGAN REPUBLICANS
AND CLINTON DEMOCRATS
ENRICHED WALL STREET
WHILE MUGGING MAIN STREET

Robert Scheer

with

Christopher Scheer *and* Joshua Scheer

NATION
BOOKS
New York

Published by Nation Books,
A Member of the Perseus Books Group
116 East 16th Street, 8th Floor
New York, NY 10003

Nation Books is a copublishing venture of the Nation Institute
and the Perseus Books Group.

Books published by Nation Books are available at special
discounts for bulk purchases in the United States by
corporations, institutions, and other organizations. For more
information, please contact the Special Markets Department at
the Perseus Books Group, 2300 Chestnut Street, Suite 200,
Philadelphia, PA 19103, or call (800) 810-4145, ext. 5000, or
e-mail special.markets@perseusbooks.com.

Set in 11.5 point Dante by the Perseus Books Group

Library of Congress Cataloging-in-Publication Data
Scheer, Robert.
  The great American stickup : how Reagan Republicans and
Clinton Democrats enriched Wall Street while mugging Main
Street / Robert Scheer with Christopher Scheer and Joshua
Scheer
  p. cm.
  Includes bibliographical references and index.
  ISBN 978-1-56858-434-8 (alk. paper)
  1. Banks and banking—Corrupt practices—United States. 2.
Financial crises—United States. I. Scheer, Christopher. II. Title.
  HG2491.S34 2010
  332.10973—dc22
                              2010017758

To my wife

NARDA ZACCHINO,

an indispensable coauthor and editor of
everything I have written for three decades,

and to my son,

PETER

Truthdig.com's managing editor, who led our staff
in winning a Webby award while I was off writing this book.

CONTENTS

CHAPTER 1

It *Was* the Economy, Stupid 1

CHAPTER 2

The High Priestess of the
Reagan Revolution 25

CHAPTER 3

The Clinton Bubble 49

CHAPTER 4

The Valiant Stand of Brooksley Born 81

CHAPTER 5

They Have No Shame 111

CHAPTER 6

Robert Rubin Rakes It In at Citigroup 139

CHAPTER 7

Poverty Pimps 169

CHAPTER 8

Goldman Cleans Up 195

CHAPTER 9

Sucking Up to the Bankers:
Crisis Handoff from Bush to Obama 215

Acknowledgments, 247

Notes, 251

Index, 273

CHAPTER I

It *Was* the Economy, Stupid

"How did this happen?"
—PRESIDENT GEORGE W. BUSH

"It was a humbling question for someone from the financial sector to be asked—after all, we were the ones responsible."
—TREASURY SECRETARY HENRY M. PAULSON JR.,
FORMER GOLDMAN SACHS CEO

They did it.

Yes, there is a "they": the captains of finance, their lobbyists, and allies among leading politicians of both parties, who together destroyed an American regulatory system that had been functioning splendidly for most of the six decades since it was enacted in the 1930s.

"They" will emerge largely unscathed—indeed, likely wealthier—from exploiting the newfound bargains in foreclosed properties and bankrupt businesses that this turmoil provides to those with access to ready cash. And even as they make taxpayers foot the bill for their grievous greed and errors, they are eager to cover their tracks and unwilling to accept responsibility for the damage done.

The big cop-out in much of what has been written about the banking meltdown has been the argument by those most complicit that there was "enough blame to go around" and that no institution or individual should be singled out for accountability. "How could we have known?" is the refrain of those who continue to pose as all-knowing experts. "Everybody made mistakes," they say.

Nonsense. This was a giant hustle that served the richest of the rich and left the rest of us holding the bag, a life-altering game of musical chairs in which the American public was the one forced out. Worst of all, legislators from both political parties we elect and pay to protect our interests from the pirates who assaulted us instead changed our laws to enable them.

The most pathetic of excuses is the one provided by Robert Rubin, who fathered "Rubinomics," the economic policy of President Clinton's two-term administration: The economy ran into a "perfect storm," a combination of unforeseen but disastrously interrelated events. This rationalization is all too readily accepted by the mass media, which is not surprising, given that it neatly absolves the majority of business reporters and editors who had missed the story for years until it was too late.

The facts are otherwise. It is not conspiratorial but rather accurate to suggest that blame can be assigned to those who consciously developed and implemented a policy of radical financial deregulation that led to a global recession. As President Clinton's Treasury secretary, Rubin, the former cochair of Goldman Sachs, led the fight to free the financial markets from regulation and then went on to a $15-million-a-year job with Citigroup, the company that had most energetically lobbied for that deregulation. He should remember the line from the old cartoon strip Pogo: "We have met the enemy and he is us."

For it was this Wall Street and Democratic Party darling, along with his clique of economist super-friends—Alan Greenspan, Lawrence Summers, and a few others—who inflated a giant real estate bubble by purposely not regulating the derivatives market, resulting in oceans of money that was poured into bad loans sold as safe investments. In the process, they not only caused an avalanche of pain and misery when the bubble inevitably burst but also shredded the good reputation of the American banking system nurtured since the Great Depression.

This book aims to describe how and why this was done, as well as who tried to stop it and why they failed, because if we accept a broad dispersal of blame or a sense of inevitability—or simply ignore the details, since they can be so confusing—we lose the opportunity to rearrange our institutions to prevent such disasters from happening again.

That this is true was only reinforced by the tentative response of the Obama administration in its first year. Even after a crash that economists agree is the biggest since the granddaddy of 1929, the president's proposed reform legislation stops far short of reintroducing the kind of regulation of the markets that prevented such disasters in the intervening eighty years. We still see a persistent fear, stoked by the same folks who led us into this abyss, that regulation and scrutiny will kill the golden goose of Wall Street profits and, by extension, U.S. prosperity.

If we as a people learn anything from this crash, however, it should be that there are no adults watching the store, only a tiny elite of self-interested multimillionaires and billionaires making decisions for the rest of us. As long as we cede that power to them, we can expect to continue getting bilked.

Three key myths consistently propagated about the financial markets proved devastating in this event. The first is that buyers and sellers are all logical and well-informed about what they are doing, so the markets will always be "corrected" to provide accurate price values. The second is that whatever happens in these "free markets," the general public will not be hurt—only irresponsible gamblers will lose their shirts. The third is that whenever the government gets involved, it will only screw things up; even if regulators only ask questions, it will poison the pond and spook the fish, to everybody's detriment.

As we will see in the following chapters, all of these assumptions were proven false; the brave new world order of super-rational high-tech derivative marketing based on Nobel Prize–winning mathematical models turned out to be a prescription for financial madness. A win-win system too good to be true turned out to be a cruel hoax in which most suffered terribly—and not just that majority of the world's population that suffers from the whims of the market, but even some who designed and sold the new financial gimmicks. Left to their own devices, freed of rational regulatory restraint by an army of lobbyists and the politicians who serve them, one after another of the very top financial conglomerates imploded from the weight of their uncontrolled greed. Or would have imploded, as in the examples of Citigroup and AIG, if the government had not used taxpayer dollars to bail out those "too big to fail" conglomerates.

Along the way, these companies—including the privatized quasi-governmental Fannie Mae and Freddie Mac monstrosities—were exposed as poorly run juggernauts, with top executives having embarrassingly little grasp of the chicanery and risk taking that was bolstering their bottom lines. Worst of all, damage from this economic chain reaction didn't, of course, stop at the bank accounts of Saudi

investors or American CEOs but led to soaring unemployment and federal debt, the acceleration of the home foreclosure epidemic, massive unemployment, and the wholesale
destruction of pension plans and state education budgets.

Since the collapse happened on the watch of President
George W. Bush at the end of two full terms in office, many
in the Democratic Party were only too eager to blame his
administration. Yet while Bush did nothing to remedy the
problem, and his response was to simply reward the culprits,
the roots of this disaster go back much further, to the free-
market propaganda of the Reagan years and, most damag-
ingly, to the bipartisan deregulation of the banking industry
undertaken with the full support of "liberal" President Clinton. Yes, Clinton. And if this debacle needs a name, it should
most properly be called "the Clinton bubble," as difficult as
it may be to accept for those of us who voted for him.

Clinton, being a smart person and an astute politician, did
not use old ideological arguments to do away with New Deal
restrictions on the banking system, which had been in place
ever since the Great Depression threatened the survival of
capitalism. His were the words of technocrats, arguing that
modern technology, globalization, and the increased sophis-
tication of traders meant the old concerns and restrictions
were outdated. By "modernizing" the economy, so the
promise went, we would free powerful creative energies and
create new wealth for a broad spectrum of Americans—not
to mention boosting the Democratic Party enormously, both
politically and financially.

And it worked: Traditional banks freed by the dissolution of New Deal regulations became much more aggressive in investing deposits, snapping up financial services companies in a binge of acquisitions. These giant conglomerates then bet long on a broad and limitless expansion of the economy, making credit easy and driving up the stock and real estate markets to unseen heights. Increasingly complicated yet wildly profitable securities—especially so-called over-the-counter derivatives (OTC), which, as their name suggests, are financial instruments derived from other assets or products—proved irresistible to global investors, even though few really understood what they were buying. Those transactions in suspect derivatives were negotiated in markets that had been freed from the obligations of government regulation and would grow in the year 2009 to more than $600 trillion.

America's middle class, excited to be trading stocks on the Internet and leveraging their homes to remodel their kitchens, approved heartily, giving Clinton seemingly irrepressible popularity even in the face of personal scandal. "It's the economy, stupid," was his famous campaign mantra, although statistics would later show that the vast majority of new wealth was going to the top 10 percent of the population. Even if real wages were basically stagnant, people felt richer, because they had what seemed to be limitless credit to enjoy the best of what the consumer culture had to offer.

Meanwhile, the Democrats had reversed a decades-long decline in fundraising might, surpassing the Republicans as

Wall Street, whose denizens tended to be socially liberal, suddenly poured money into the party's coffers. This trend continues today: President Obama's second-biggest contributor was the investment bank Goldman Sachs, which played a key role in the economic collapse even as, with the government's help, it survived and went on to new heights of profit.

The good times, however, were based on a foundation of sand. At the boom's heart was a casino in which everyone was seemingly betting one way—even as they were buying insurance on their bets, which allowed them to believe they were playing it safe. This virtual market was a huge expansion in derivatives futures trading, transforming a market based on predicting the prices of well-understood commodities into the realm of financial hocus-pocus. Unlike the traditional staple products—pork bellies, wheat, and other such commodities—of the major futures exchange, these new products were more varied, less transparent, and almost completely unregulated. The new derivatives were sold over the counter—instead of on a public exchange—meaning that a buyer and a seller simply made deals directly. But what was really different about these OTC derivatives that caused the meltdown was what the investors were buying: future payments and/or interest on debts.

Here's how it worked: Initial lenders—banks, savings and loans, credit companies—would give out money to consumers or businesses to purchase equipment, inventory, credit cards, cars, and boats, but mostly mortgages on houses and commercial real estate. Investment banks would then buy these "debt obligations" in "bundles" worth hundreds of millions of dollars. Using complex mathematical formulas, they would then sort the contents of a bundle by the predicted risks.

Those risks involved either default on loan obligations or the prepayment of loans by consumers to avoid interest obligations. In either case, the flow of interest income—the basis of the bundled derivatives—would be compromised. To avoid such losses, the bundles of derivatives would be sliced and diced into "tranches" (French for slices), in which investors, especially huge institutional buyers, could more easily invest. Oh, and they would pay an ostensibly neutral rating agency to validate that the risk level was as advertised.

As if this wasn't enough of a complicated novelty, another angle was linked to this market: swaps. This was a form of insurance, or so it appeared to those who paid for it, that would protect investors if things went so sour that folks stopped paying back their debts. AIG, for example, once a traditional and regulated insurance provider, suddenly started making wild profits backing up bad debts on those credit derivatives. As opposed to their traditional insurance, however, these "swaps" were not regulated. And when the collapse occurred, it happened that AIG had not put aside sufficient funds to back these obligations. Your taxpayer dollars, $180 billion worth, were used instead.

Beginning in the early '90s, this innovative system for buying and selling debt grew from a boutique, almost experimental, Wall Street business model to something so large that, when it collapsed a little more than a decade later, it would cause a global recession. Along the way, as we will see, only a few people possessed enough knowledge and integrity to point out that the growth and profits it was generating were, in fact, too good to be true.

Until it all fell apart in such grand fashion, turning some of the most prestigious companies in the history of capitalism into bankrupt beggars, all the key players in the derivatives markets were happy as pigs in excrement. At the bottom, a plethora of aggressive lenders was only too happy to sign up folks for mortgages and other loans they could not afford because those loans could be bundled and sold in the market as collateralized debt obligations (CDOs). The investment banks were thrilled to have those new CDOs to sell, their clients liked the absurdly high returns being paid— even if they really had no clear idea what they were buying— and the "swap" sellers figured they were taking no risk at all, since the economy seemed to have entered a phase in which it had only one direction: up.

Of course, this was ridiculous on the face of it. Could it really be so easy? What was the catch? Never mind that, you spoiler! Not only were those making the millions and billions off the OTC derivatives market ecstatic, so were the politicians, bought off by Wall Street, who were sitting in the driver's seat while the bubble was inflating. With credit so easy, consumers went on a binge, buying everything in sight, which in turn was a boon to the bricks-and-mortar economy.

Blown upward by all this "irrational exuberance," as then Federal Reserve Bank chair Alan Greenspan noted in one of his more honest moments, the stock market soared, creating the era of e-trade and a middle class that eagerly awaited each quarterly 401(k) report.

Later, in the rubble, consumer borrowers would be scapegoated for the crash. This is the same logic as blaming passengers of a discount airline for their deaths if it turned out the plane had been flown by a monkey. Shouldn't they have known they should pay more? In reality, the gushing profits of the collateralized debt markets meant the original lenders had no motive to actually vet the recipients—they wouldn't be trying to collect the debt themselves anyway. Instead, they would do almost anything to entreat consumers to borrow far beyond their means, reassuring them in a booming economy they'd be suckers not to buy, buy, buy.

That this madness was allowed to develop without significant government supervision or critical media interest, despite the inherent instability and predictable future damage of a system of growth predicated on its own inevitability, is a tribute to the almost limitless power of Wall Street lobbyists and the corruption of political leaders who did their bidding while sacrificing the public's interest.

While much has been made of the baffling complexity of the new market structures at the heart of the banking meltdown, there were informed and prescient observers who in real time saw through these gimmicks. The potential for damage was thus known inside the halls of power to those who cared to know, if only because of heroes like gutsy regulator Brooksley Born, chair of the Commodity Futures Trading Commission from 1996 to 1999. When they attempted to sound the alarm, however, they were ignored, or worse. Simply put, the rewards in both financial remuneration and advanced careers were such that those in a position to profit went along with great enthusiasm. Those who objected, like Born, were summarily crushed.

What follows in this book is the story of those who acted in the public interest and attempted to prevent this unfolding disaster and the response of a far more powerful coterie of ideologically driven and yet avaricious government and business leaders. By and large, those leaders have not been held accountable for their actions and, indeed, most often went on to reap even greater rewards as born-again reformers called upon to set right that which they had wrecked. Far too many have been granted far-reaching powers in President Barack Obama's administration as foxes told to fix the damage they themselves have done to the henhouse.

Of the leaders responsible, five names come prominently to mind: Alan Greenspan, the longtime head of the Federal Reserve; Robert Rubin, who served as Treasury secretary in the Clinton administration; Lawrence Summers, who succeeded him in that capacity; and the two top Republicans in Congress back in the 1990s dealing with finance, Phil Gramm and James Leach.

Arrayed most prominently against them, far, far down the DC power ladder, were two female regulators, Born and Sheila Bair (an appointee of Bush I and II and retained as FDIC chair by Obama). They never had a chance, though; they were facing a juggernaut: The combined power of the Wall Street lobbyists allied with popular President Clinton, who staked his legacy on reassuring the titans of finance a Democrat could serve their interests better than any Republican.

Clinton's role was decisive in turning Ronald Reagan's obsession with an unfettered free market into law. Reagan, that fading actor recast so effectively as great propagandist for the unregulated market—"get government off our backs" was his signature rallying cry—was far more successful at deregulating smokestack industries than the financial markets. It would take a new breed of "triangulating" technocrat Democrats to really dismantle the carefully built net designed, after the last Great Depression, to restrain Wall Street from its pattern of periodic self-immolations.

Even some of the brightest liberals, such as Nobel Prize–winning economist Paul Krugman, have failed to realize how their party, long claiming to represent the middle and working classes, did so much to let the smart money guys run us all into the ground. "The prime villains behind the mess we're in were Reagan and his circle of advisers," Krugman wrote in a June 2009 column, perhaps out of wishful thinking. Reagan's 1982 signing of the Garn–St. Germain Depository Institutions Act easing mortgage interest requirements pales in comparison to the damage wrought fifteen years later by the collateralized debt bubble, which couldn't have existed but for a series of key deregulatory laws pushed through during the Clinton years with the president's support.

This process was neither an accident nor an oversight; at the center of Clinton's strategy for political success was the much commented-on "triangulation" that sought to avoid the traditional liberal-conservative divide on issues by finding a win-win solution that appropriated the most politically appealing elements of competing approaches. Nowhere during the eight years of the Clinton presidency was that triangulation strategy applied with greater energy than toward economic policy.

But while the strategy appeared to work wonderfully and the administration was praised widely for having presided over what Clinton often referred to as the longest sustained period of prosperity in American history, it no longer can be logically viewed that way after the banking meltdown. Instead of sustained prosperity, the U.S. economy had created an enormous bubble, based on rampant borrowing and speculation, that inevitably burst, as all bubbles do. And whereas Clinton would brag that his management of the economy had embraced the needs of Wall Street as well as the vast majority, including those at the lower end of the economic scale, it ended up performing well only for those already at the top.

Analyzing U.S. tax data and other supporting statistics, UC Berkeley economist Emmanuel Saez and his colleague

Thomas Piketty concluded that the boom of the Clinton years and afterward primarily benefitted the wealthiest Americans. During Clinton's tenure—from 1993 to 2000— the income of the top 1 percent shot up at the astounding rate of 10.1 percent per year, while the income of the other 99 percent of Americans increased only 2.4 percent annually. In 2002–2006, the next surge of the boom that Clinton's policies unleashed, the numbers were even more unbalanced: The average annual income for the bottom 99 percent increased by only 1 percent per annum, while the top 1 percent saw a gain of 11 percent each year.

Further, just as the good times of the Bush years saw almost $3 out of every $4 in increased income go to the wealthiest 1 percent, the GOP cut taxes for the richest brackets. An understanding of why the nation's media and political elites failed to question the Clinton claim of prosperity may be found in the fact that almost all of them were in the elite that benefitted, having had pretax family income higher than the $104,700 that qualified for the top 10 percent category in 2006, and some made more than the $382,600 to be included in the top 1 percent.

Presumably, had the boom continued, some would have argued that the rapid enrichment of the top 1 percent would have been justified by the increases in the real worth of the bottom 99 percent. But the boom didn't continue, and with the crash came unfathomable loss across the board. By June 2009, the Federal Reserve reported that the net worth of

U.S. households had dropped for seven straight quarters, with families losing 22 percent of the wealth that they had obtained by the spring of 2007. Most of that loss occurred in the declining value of homes and stocks in retirement programs.

And nobody was predicting that all that paper wealth was going to come back in a hurry—or perhaps ever at all. "I don't think the worst is over," Lawrence Summers, who was Clinton's Treasury secretary and who would reemerge as the top economic adviser in the Obama White House, told the *Financial Times* on July 10, 2009. "It's very likely that more jobs will be lost. It would not be surprising if GDP has not yet reached its low. What does appear to be true is that the sense of panic in the markets and freefall in the economy has subsided, and one does not have the sense of a situation as out of control as a few months ago."

Some experts were less sanguine. Former Clinton administration Labor secretary Robert Reich believes there is no going back to the way things were. "In a recession this deep, recovery doesn't depend on investors," wrote Reich on his blog on July 9, 2009. "It depends on consumers who, after all, are 70% of the US economy. And this time consumers got really whacked." Reich continues:

> Until consumers start spending again, you can forget any recovery . . . Problem is . . . they don't have the money, and it's hard to see where it will come from.

They can't borrow. Their homes are worth a fraction
of what they were before, so say goodbye to home equity loans and refinancings. One out of ten homeowners is under water—owing more on their homes than
their homes are worth. Unemployment continues to
rise, and number of hours at work continues to drop.
Those who can are saving. Those who can't are hun-
kering down, as they must . . . And don't rely on ex-
ports. The global economy is contracting. My
prediction, then? Not a V, not a U. But an X. This economy can't get back on track because the track we were
on for years—featuring flat or declining median
wages, mounting consumer debt, and widening inse-
curity, not to mention increasing carbon in the atmosphere—simply cannot be sustained.

What Reich was suggesting was that there would be neither a sharp ("V") nor a more gradual ("U") return to the
high rolling times before the balloon burst. Instead, we have
entered a very different economy in which high-paying jobs
and the appearance of lower-middle-class prosperity might
not return ("X").

Into this mess stepped Barack Obama, after his historic
election as America's first African American president. Early
in the campaign, Obama had shown a sophisticated grasp of
the causes of the crash, and one in line with the central thesis
of this book. Speaking at Manhattan's Cooper Union on

March 27, 2008, the Democratic Primary candidate provided
what still stands as one of the best analyses of the extent and
causes of the economic crisis:

> The American experiment has worked in large part
> because we have guided the market's invisible hand
> with a higher principle. Our free market was never
> meant to be a free license to take whatever you can
> get, however you can get it. That is why we have put
> in place rules of the road to make competition fair,
> and open, and honest. We have done this not to sti-
> fle—but rather to advance prosperity and liberty. As I
> said at NASDAQ last September: the core of our eco-
> nomic success is the fundamental truth that each
> American does better when all Americans do better;
> that the well-being of American business, its capital
> markets, and the American people are aligned. I think
> all of us here today would acknowledge that we've lost
> that sense of shared prosperity.

What has been undermined was the wisdom of Franklin
Delano Roosevelt's New Deal reforms that capitalism
needed to be saved from its own excess in order to survive,
that the free market would remain free only if it was properly regulated in the public interest. The great and terrible
irony of capitalism is that if left unfettered, it inexorably en-
gineers its own demise, through either revolution or eco-

nomic collapse. The guardians of capitalism's survival are thus not the self-proclaimed free-marketers, who, in defiance of the pragmatic Adam Smith himself, want to chop away at all government restraints on corporate actions, but rather liberals, at least those in the mode of FDR, who seek to harness its awesome power while keeping its workings palatable to a civilized and progressive society.

Government regulation of the market economy arose during the New Deal out of a desire to save capitalism rather than destroy it. Whether it was child labor in dark coal mines, the exploitation of racially segregated human beings to pick cotton, or the unfathomable devastation of the Great Depression, the brutal creativity of the pure profit motive has always posed a stark challenge to our belief that we are moral creatures. The modern bureaucratic governments of the developed world were built, unconsciously, as a bulwark, something big enough to occasionally stand up to the power of uncontrolled market forces, much as a referee must show the yellow card to a young headstrong athlete. So what kind of ref would Obama prove to be? While it is far too early to establish his legacy, so far he seems to be the kind who talks a better game than he calls.

At the time of the Cooper Union speech, when the candidate's main opponent in the Democratic primary was the wife of the Democratic president who had signed off on radical deregulation of those free markets, Obama was heeding some economic experts who early on had disassociated themselves from the policy of President Clinton. His most prominent business adviser was Warren Buffett, who as early as 2002 had condemned OTC derivatives as "financial weapons of mass destruction."

Later, after the Illinois senator defeated Hillary Clinton, almost all of the old Bill Clinton economic team, only slightly chastened by the collapse of their bubble, would, astonishingly, come to dominate Obama's campaign and future administration. But at that moment, in March 2008, while still neck and neck with Senator Clinton in the race for the Democratic nomination, Obama's remarks were an explicit denunciation of Clinton's Rubinomics. The key to Rubinomics, really just a series of gifts to Wall Street elites, was the radical deregulation of the financial markets that this former Goldman Sachs executive pushed as Clinton's Treasury secretary.

Rubin, by then one of the top three leaders of Citigroup, the company that had most benefitted from the 1990s deregulation binge and that subsequently would be disgraced by the greed it turned loose, also had spoken at Cooper Union—two months earlier, in January 2008. At that point, Rubin was advising the Hillary Clinton campaign and was spoken of as a possible vice presidential candidate, and he offered only blithe optimism of what he defined as the noncrisis we were experiencing. Coverage by CNNMoney.com and *Fortune* magazine was headlined "Robert Rubin: What Meltdown?" with the subhead, "In a talk on Wednesday, the Citigroup director said the current financial upheaval is just

cyclical. And none of the blame that there was to assign went
to Wall Street."

The extent to which Rubin, despite his reputation as an
economic wise man, was out of touch with the emerging
reality was revealed in journalist Katie Benner's report:

> A lending catastrophe has consumed homeowners,
> mortgage companies, and the financial system, but
> Robert Rubin, Citigroup's director and executive com-
> mittee chair, doesn't seem particularly alarmed.
>
> He told a small crowd at Manhattan's Cooper
> Union for the Advancement of Science and Art
> Wednesday that the problems now roiling the markets
> and forcing the Federal Reserve into a defensive pos-
> ture are "all part of a cycle of periodic excess leading
> to periodic disruption," and that we are not in fact on
> the verge of a financial meltdown.
>
> And the economic problems that he did acknowl-
> edge were blamed on just about everyone but the
> major US financial players.
>
> Rubin said part of the problem is that we need a
> "more educated electorate" to hold politicians ac-
> countable.

Rubin's remarks were bizarrely out of touch with a financial world that was already in freefall. In his own speech two
months later, Obama was anything but glib, as he spoke mov-
ingly of the pain from loss of jobs and homes that already

had occurred and warned correctly that it would get a lot worse. He also was uncharacteristically blunt about where the blame for the economy's collapse should be placed. It is repeated here at some length, for it could serve as the theme for this book and provides a yardstick by which to measure the new president's subsequent course of action:

> This loss has not happened by accident. It's because of decisions made in boardrooms, on trading floors, and in Washington. Under Republican and Democratic administrations, we failed to guard against practices that all too often rewarded financial manipulation instead of productivity and sound business practices. We let the special interests put their thumbs on the economic scales.
>
> The result has been a distorted market that creates bubbles instead of steady, sustainable growth, a market that favors Wall Street over Main Street but ends up hurting both. Nor is this trend new. The concentrations of economic power—and the failures of our political system to protect the American economy from its worst excesses—have been a staple of our past, most famously in the 1920s, when such excesses ultimately plunged the country into the Great Depression. That is when government stepped in to create a series of regulatory structures—from the FDIC to the Glass-Steagall Act—to serve as a corrective to protect the American people and American business.

Instead of reasonable changes in regulation that protected the public interest while acknowledging the changes in trading and other aspects of doing business in a high-tech trading world, the reversal of the regulatory protections of Glass-Steagall took steps to wreck the economy rather than improve it. Unfortunately, Obama would end up turning to the very people who in the Clinton administration had led the fight to repeal the New Deal regulations. But back then, in his speech, he took the proper measure of their folly:

> Unfortunately, instead of establishing a 21st century regulatory framework, we simply dismantled the old one—aided by a legal but corrupt bargain in which campaign money all too often shaped policy and watered down oversight. In doing so, we encouraged a winner take all, anything goes environment that helped foster devastating dislocations in our economy.
>
> Deregulation of the telecommunications sector, for example, fostered competition but also contributed to massive over-investment. Partial deregulation of the electricity sector enabled market manipulation. Companies like Enron and WorldCom took advantage of the new regulatory environment to push the envelope, pump up earnings, disguise losses, and otherwise engage in accounting fraud to make their profits look better—a practice that led investors to question the balance sheet of all companies, and severely damaged public trust in capital markets. This was not the

invisible hand at work. Instead, it was the hand of industry lobbyists tilting the playing field in Washington, an accounting industry that had developed
powerful conflicts of interest, and a financial sector
that fueled over-investment.

A decade later, we have deregulated the financial
services sector, and we face another crisis . . . When
subprime mortgage lending took a reckless and un-
sustainable turn, a patchwork of regulators was un-
able or unwilling to protect the American people.

That's about as good a big-picture takeout as you can find
on what went wrong, and one of the mysteries to be explored in this book is why Obama's early vision on these
matters did not inform his actions as president.

A tip-off to the answer might be that the lobbying
forces—the power of that massive wealth to control politics
which Obama in his speech referred to as "the $300 million
lobbying effort that drove deregulation"—did not stop functioning with the election of Barack Obama to the presidency,
and that to some degree, even a politician who read the danger signs so well could succumb to the very forces that he
had earlier decried.

CHAPTER 2

The High Priestess of the Reagan Revolution

Ronald Reagan called her his favorite economist, and Wendy Lee Gramm seemed to deserve the praise. Both while she was an academic economist and after Reagan appointed her to various regulatory positions in his administration, she excelled in articulating antiregulatory rhetoric that marked her as a true believer in what would later be labeled the "Reagan Revolution."

Reagan himself had risen in politics after eight years of tutelage as a spokesman for the General Electric Company, from 1954 to 1962. It was a time of conversion, as he described it, from being a "hemophiliac liberal" Hollywood actor to a cold-blooded Big Business conservative. Carrying the company's banner, Reagan came to absorb the message that government regulation developed during the New Deal had become a chokehold on economic growth.

Although as governor of California and later in the White House Reagan would preside over massive government budgets and even expand them, he found in Gramm an ideological "small government" soul mate. The Mercatus Center, an antiregulation think tank based at George Mason University from which Gramm has proselytized mightily, proudly boasts in her website biography that the *Wall Street Journal* "called her 'The Margaret Thatcher of financial regulation.'"

However, unlike the former British prime minister, neither Gramm nor President Reagan was able to bring about much change in the balance between government and the private sector. While his administration did funnel hundreds of billions of dollars in new Cold War military spending to corporate contractors—hugely expanding the national debt in the process—Reagan was not able to deliver to Wall Street a parallel windfall.

For Wall Street, the holy grail was not cash handouts but a deconstruction of the complex public-private partnership ushered in by Franklin Roosevelt's New Deal to restrain capitalism's most self-destructive patterns. For these so-called FIRE firms—Finance, Insurance, and Real Estate—this half-

century-old regulatory system, modest as it was, was an ir-
ritant that limited their ability to gamble and leverage their
dominant positions.

While the companies just wanted to be free of restraint
to profit at will, Reagan and Gramm were true believers, arguing that the regulatory status quo was outmoded and
onerous—even socialist—hobbling business growth. The
top target in their sights was the New Deal–enacted Glass-
Steagall Act of 1933, signed into law by President Roosevelt,
which regulated the financial services industry. Key to its ef-
fectiveness was the seemingly simple wall it erected between
the commercial banks entrusted with depositors' funds—
and insured by the government's Federal Deposit Insurance
Corporation (FDIC), the agency created by Glass-Steagall—
and the wilder antics of basically unregulated Wall Street investment banks like Goldman Sachs.

In 1982, Reagan signed the Garn–St. Germain Depository
Institutions Act, easing regulation of savings and loans and,
in the eyes of critics such as Paul Krugman, paving the way
for the S&L collapse in the 1980s as well as the subprime
housing crisis decades later. Nevertheless, Reagan made
clear even then that this was not the biggest target on his
list:

> Unfortunately, this legislation does not deal with the
> important question of delivery of other services,
> including securities activities by banks and other

depository institutions. But I'm advised that many in the Congress want to put this question at the top of the banking deregulatory agendas next year, and I would strongly endorse such an initiative and hope that at the same time, the Congress will consider other proposals for more comprehensive deregulation which the administration advanced during the 97th Congress.

Reagan's timeline, however, was overly optimistic; economic problems, particularly the savings and loan meltdown and the spiraling national debt, made politicians of both parties cautious. Yet, in one of the grand twists of American politics, the proposals he sought would eventually be signed into law more than a decade later by a Democratic president with a reputation of being a liberal child of the 1960s. In fact, at the end of Reagan's presidency, Congress passed legislation that *toughened* rather than weakened financial industry regulation. As *Time* magazine reported on August 17, 1987:

> Ronald Reagan's dream of carrying out a sweeping deregulation of the US economy has stirred a powerful backlash on Capitol Hill. Never has that been more apparent than last week, when Congress passed its first comprehensive piece of banking legislation since 1982. The White House had hoped the bill would remove

many of the governmental shackles that inhibit competition between banks, securities firms and other institutions in the burgeoning field of financial services.
In fact, it does just the opposite.

Reagan signed the bill, the Competitive Equality Banking
Act of 1987, only after criticizing it for not only failing to
tear down the Glass-Steagall walls but, worse, temporarily
extending "the 1933 Glass-Steagall Act restrictions on securities activities to state-chartered, non-member banks for
the first time." He made it clear he was signing the bill despite his quite vociferous objections because it contained
provisions for funding for local banks in trouble. It was at
once a statement of the enormous importance he attached
to decimating Glass-Steagall and an admission that he
would come to the end of his last term without accomplish-
ing that goal.

So legislatively his administration was a bust when it
came to reversing the New Deal. Yet rhetorically it was an
enormous success in propagandizing a view that so-called
big government was the cause of America's late-twentieth-
century crisis of economic confidence. He managed to pop-
ularize and make palatable the heretofore fringe belief that
government regulation of the financial sector, rather than
saving capitalism from itself, was an irrational hindrance to
individual profit and even a threat to our national power.
Speaking at the signing of the 1987 bill, Reagan noted,

"These new anti-consumer and anti-competitive provisions could hold back a vital service industry at a time when competition in the international capital markets increasingly challenges United States financial institutions, and they should be repealed."

With great political irony, this speech would be repeated almost word for word a dozen years later, when Democrat Bill Clinton reversed a half century of his party's core economic principles to argue for the repeal of Glass-Steagall. Clinton's public rationale for this watershed shift was that if regulation of Wall Street were not "modernized"—political code for weakened or eliminated—the United States would lose out to foreign competition in capital markets.

Much of the groundwork for Clinton's break was laid by the diligent Republican Wendy Lee Gramm and her husband, Senator Phil Gramm, also a Texas Republican. The high priestess and priest of financial deregulation met at a conference in New York, where Wendy Lee, a PhD student in economics, was interviewing with Phil Gramm for a position at Texas A&M University, where he was a senior professor. Wendy Gramm would later tell interviewers that as Professor Gramm was helping her on with her coat at the interview's conclusion, he expressed interest in dating her if she came to Texas. She later told the *New York Times* her reaction to him was "Oh, yuck," but Gramm persisted, and six weeks after she arrived on campus, they wed.

His bold self-confidence might have helped carry the duo as apostles of an unabashedly Big Business creed then increasingly gaining currency in academic economic circles and within both political parties. Back in 1976, in fact, Jimmy Carter, now known mostly for his postpresidency activism on behalf of Third World democracy, Middle East peace, and ending poverty in America, was a strong advocate of business deregulation. As Georgia's governor, Carter had been a fiscal conservative who, in the tradition of conservative Southern Democrats, shunned Northern liberalism.

Phil Gramm, too, came out of that tradition. After obtaining his doctorate in economics from the University of Georgia in 1967, the year after Carter lost his first bid to be that state's governor, Gramm moved on to Texas A&M and taught economics for twelve years before jumping into politics. Gramm was elected to Congress as a Democrat in 1978; just three years later, he would become the epitome of a "Reagan Democrat" by cosponsoring the Gramm-Latta budget that implemented Reagan's economic program. Proudly, at his retirement from the Senate, Gramm cooed, "in 1981, I wrote the first Reagan budget."

Gramm then abruptly resigned from the U.S. House of Representatives on February 12, 1983, forcing a special election for his seat, and the next month was elected to that seat as a Republican. After serving a third term, he completed his meteoric rise by being elected to the Senate in 1984. Until he retired, he would prove to be arguably the most influential Republican on financial issues.

As chair of the Senate's Banking, Housing, and Urban Affairs Committee from 1995 to 2000, he was in a position, with Clinton's support, to finally make Reagan's commitment to radical deregulation of the financial markets a reality. This was accomplished with two signature pieces of legislation that he—surely more than anyone else—was responsible for putting into the law books: the Financial Services Modernization Act of 1999 and the Commodity Futures Modernization Act of 2000.

Certainly there were many other legislators and bureaucrats pushing for what was euphemistically called "banking reform." By now the FIRE industries were pumping hundreds of millions of dollars into each major election cycle to lobby both parties to support the reversal of Glass-Steagall's regulatory provisions and similar regulations, and so they had plenty of eager helpers. With union membership on the decline in America, Democrats decided they no longer could let Wall Street money flow in such unequal measure to Republicans; under Clinton's lead, the floodgates of campaign payola were now fully bipartisan.

Senator Gramm's committee status and long-term persistence on the matter, however, gave him alpha status: The legislation that finally would reverse the venerable Glass-Steagall laws would carry his name first: the Gramm-Leach-

Bliley Act, which would be signed into law as the Financial Services Modernization Act of 1999. However, some years before Glass-Steagall was dismantled, Phil's wife played a key role, as a member of both the Reagan and the Bush I administrations, in shaping the rapid changes in the financial markets brought about by internationalization, computer-driven trading, and the introduction of a whole new discipline of "risk management," whereby Wall Street wizards deployed complex mathematical models to create a vast array of new financial products, such as the now infamous credit default swaps and collateralized debt obligations.

As was seen throughout the Reagan and later the Bush I and Bush II administrations, the Republicans had realized they could impose de facto deregulation of Big Business by appointing to influential federal commissions and agencies "watchdogs" who were sympathetic to the corporations they were supposed to be monitoring. Of course, this end run around congressional authority was probably not as satisfying or foolproof as wiping out the regulation altogether, yet it proved quite effective in pleasing CEOs, who had spent the 1970s complaining about red tape and overzealous government investigators.

Thus it was that professional deregulation activist Wendy Gramm came to be appointed by Reagan as chair of the Commodity Futures Trading Commission in 1988, which was the governmental arm most likely to regulate those newfangled investment devices that seemed so much like futures. Gramm, who would never think of questioning any of these clever "modern" gimmicks, saw them as an unmitigated blessing.

Rather than destabilizing the world economy, as they would prove to do two decades later, these products were supposed to be a win-win that would increase market efficiency by bringing order to pricing and the management of risk. Greater productivity, lower prices, and enormous new sources of wealth would inevitably follow. Of course, the top echelon of Wall Street insiders would skim the cream off, but, the argument went, the rest of the country would benefit as well. Not only would the economy be stronger, but American individuals, pension plans, and charities could all ride this dragon skyward, through investments and through donations from the mega-rich looking for tax shelters. It is no accident, then, that in each of the recent economic collapses, from Enron to Bernie Madoff, there arose the ever-present laments from charities that were suddenly defunded.

The derivatives and swaps involved buying and packaging financial risk and selling it based on a system of corresponding grades. So a bank might buy up a collection of mortgages or credit card debts from lenders, who could then take this capital to bankroll even more loans. The buyers of this securitized debt would sort and slice it into levels of predicted risk; the more risk, the higher the return, of course. A buyer in this still small but expanding market could then "insure" this risk—for a price.

The end result by the turn of the century was a massive casino in which bettors poured money into huge gambles on expected gain or to hedge against a loss if conditions changed. Think Las Vegas—only this market was unregulated instead of being supervised by government agencies, the same way we regulate bets made on gambling tables or the future price of products such as wheat, pork bellies, or oil on regulated commodity exchanges. Such regulations increase transparency and accuracy in the description of the commodity, the terms of trade in their future, and the accountability of the parties involved.

Wendy Gramm, however, disagreed. As chair of the Commodity Futures Trading Commission from 1988 to 1993, she did everything, perhaps more than anyone else in America, to quash valid concerns about this burgeoning market in derivatives. At the start of her term, the trading of securitized debt based on mortgages of questionable value—so-called subprime lending—barely existed, yet by the end of her tenure it was an emerging force, and alarm bells were going off in economic circles.

The journal *American Banker* acknowledged these concerns in an article focusing on Gramm's response to this situation. "Soothing Words About Derivatives: Futures Regulator Says Risks Have Been Exaggerated" was the September 21, 1992, headline. What followed in the report of a Wendy Gramm speech was her confident dismissal of the concerns expressed by others in government about a market that seemed to have come from nowhere and was growing exponentially.

"Lately, I've been hearing various regulators raise concerns about off-exchange markets and about derivatives generally," Gramm is quoted as saying. "The questions they're raising include: Are derivative markets too big, too risky, placing the clearing system in jeopardy? Are derivatives and their risks simply too esoteric and complex for anyone but a rocket scientist to understand? Are the derivative markets under-regulated?"

Those were intended as rhetorical questions and dismissed in the negative by Gramm. She claimed there wasn't that much money involved, anyway: "First, there is [the] notion that the size of the derivatives market could disrupt the financial system. When people talk about swaps, we often hear figures in trillions of dollars," she said. Gramm emphasized that the actual value of the debt—as opposed to the spiraling quantity of offsetting bets and hedges on the value—was much more modest, and thus nothing to worry about.

If only. Five years later, the notional value of OTC derivatives had grown to $24 trillion, and after another ten years, when the meltdown occurred, we would be talking about $640 trillion in the notional value of all unregulated derivative trading.

As for those "swaps" to which Gramm referred, scoffing at alarmists who thought "trillions" were at stake and that the swaps could "disrupt the financial system"—boy, did they ever. "The Monster That Ate Wall Street: How 'credit default swaps'—an insurance against bad loans—turned from a smart bet into a killer" was the title and subheading of a *Newsweek* article on October 6, 2008, referring to credit default swaps, "which ballooned into a $62 trillion market . . . nearly four times the value of all stock traded on the New York Stock Exchange."

Of course in hindsight, Gramm's glibness, whether cynical or naïve, seems patently absurd; the worrywarts were completely right. Clearly, as legislators across the board in the United States and the European Union have indicated with their votes on new regulations, the derivatives markets were not just underregulated but in no significant way regulated at all. Yet it is important to pay attention to Wendy Gramm's arguments back then because they in fact carried the day, resulting in the passage eight years later—at her senator husband's instigation—of the Commodity Futures Modernization Act, which would enshrine into law the Gramms' hands-off approach to the derivatives market de jure. The CFMA's blanket ban on any regulation by any government agency of these suspect derivatives could be seen as taking direct aim at Wendy Gramm's successor as commission chair, Brooksley Born, who would dare to raise significant questions about the soundness of these products.

One reason traders probably feared regulation is that clarity about what the derivatives really contained would have severely deflated the market for them. The complexity of the computer-driven models both obscured and validated the risks buyers were taking in buying a tranche or slice of a bundle of collected credit obligations. Amid complexity compounded by swap agreements to reduce risk, investors acted as if they'd found the alchemical secret to earning huge returns, not realizing they were simply riding a bubble that would eventually rupture with terrifying force.

Wendy Gramm, however, argued that the system was simple and logical. "As to the concern that derivatives are too esoteric, and the perception that derivatives are overcomplicated and too difficult to price: Well, you and I know that the pricing of many derivatives is simple and understood," she claimed in her speech. "Moreover, some are making the point that as banks begin to value loan portfolios the way they value derivatives, they're doing a better job of assessing risks."

Only they weren't. On the contrary, as anybody not living in a cave now knows, the giant banks, led by executives and boards seeking fast profits, joined in a mad feeding frenzy, gobbling up so-called liars' loans given out willy-nilly by off-brand lenders that are almost all now bankrupt. In light of today's knowledge, Wendy Gramm seems not to have understood what was happening all around her. It is difficult not to laugh at her final assurance that regulators were in place to keep order in this new market.

"Finally, the idea that derivatives are unregulated or insufficiently regulated: I frequently have to remind people that the CFTC does regulate exchange-traded commodity futures and options, while the SEC regulates options on equities," she said in her speech covered by *American Banker*. "While off-exchange derivatives may not be directly regulated by a government agency, the entity offering these instruments or acting as an intermediary for the products is often regulated . . . Besides, markets used by sophisticated, informed institutions tend to develop their own system of safeguards and protections."

Not a word of that turned out to be true; in fact, it already had been proved wrong at the time she spoke. The CFTC, thanks to rulings pushed through by Gramm, did not have the power to regulate so-called over-the-counter derivatives, and when Brooksley Born later tried to assert some new rules to accomplish that, Gramm, now working in the private sector, attacked her efforts. Gramm testified on July 17, 1998, before a congressional committee that Born's concern was misplaced. Whereas previously she had said critics were exaggerating the size of the OTC market, she now took its wild growth to be proof that not regulating it had been the right decision all along.

Wendy Gramm, by then on the board of Enron, and the director of the aforementioned Mercatus Center that Enron would help fund, was as proud as could be of a new financial world that she had done much to create six years before, when she was in the government. She had, largely on her own as chair of the Commodity Futures Trading

Commission, reversed what existed of efforts to regulate the financial derivatives market. Prior to her chairing the commission, that market had not been much of a factor in the U.S. economy. And what *did* exist in the way of financial derivatives had been tightly regulated by a law passed in 1974 that created the commission, which stated that financial futures must be treated the way futures of agricultural products had been dealt with in recognized exchanges.

As trading practices internationally became more reliant on computerized mathematical models, there was pressure to develop new means of sharing the risk in the trade of commodities beyond agriculture. The new action concerned financial instruments tied to swings in prices on everything from currency variations to interest rates on home mortgages. That activity mushroomed through deals between private parties that were not regulated by commodity trading exchanges. Somewhat alarmed, the CFTC, even with a Reagan-appointed chair, had proposed a rule in December 1987, the year before Gramm took over, that tightened regulations. The proposal was that the new financial swaps and hybrid instruments that were becoming more common should be regulated by exchanges. Stopping that proposed rule change and any others that would regulate the market became Gramm's crusade.

Through a series of rules by the commission, once she took over, and the 1992 passage by Congress of a law that Gramm endorsed, the burgeoning market in financial derivatives was effectively protected from regulation and allowed to spin off into fifteen years of wild growth, culminating in the debacle of 2007, when those same financial products began to self-destruct. That progression of events is not in question, and indeed the historical trajectory was boasted about by Wendy Gramm in congressional testimony on July 17, 1998, when she attacked the efforts of Brooksley Born, who had dared issue a "Concept Release" suggesting a need to regulate that market:

> Much has been said about the growth of the OTC swaps market, especially since 1993, when regulations concerning swaps and other OTC instruments were finalized pursuant to the Futures Trading Practices Act of 1992 (FTPA). The CFTC has stated in its "concept release" that it is reviewing regulations in part because of the rapid growth and changes in the marketplace during the past five years.
>
> I think it important to point out that this growth is not surprising. Indeed, the objective of the swaps provision in the FTPA along with the earlier Swaps Policy Statement, hybrid regulations and related statutory interpretations was to provide some regulatory and jurisdictional guidance in order to ensure that these markets could and would develop. In other words, these markets developed because we established some clear lines and removed some of the regulatory clouds

that hampered development of these markets in the United States. Indeed, we should be surprised if these markets had NOT grown.

Yes, the OTC market was growing fast—like a malignant tumor. We now know that this financial cancer would become a terribly destructive force for hundreds of millions of people. Yet by then, in 1998, Gramm was not alone in missing the signs of impending disaster, a lonely voice left over from the Reagan era. No, her views were aligned perfectly not only with her powerful senator husband's but with those of the Clinton administration and its Wall Street–dominated economic team that had come to power. The Reagan Revolution had found a comfortable new home among the Democrats.

The irony is that the deregulatory changes that Wendy Gramm fought for during the Reagan years and afterward under the first President Bush, along with the work of her powerful husband, led eventually in 2008–2009 to a vast increase of government control of the financial markets after they collapsed. If one looks back on her career in government spanning two presidents, before she moved on to positions on various corporate boards—most infamously Enron's, prior to that company's ignominious collapse—it is most accurate to think of her as having unwittingly subverted rather than enhanced Reagan's legacy of faith in an unfettered private economy.

After the meltdown, there was widespread demand in the United States and abroad for much tighter regulation of financial markets. That push for a greater government role came about as a result of the unbridled greed of corporate executives who exploited their newfound freedom to enrich themselves at the expense of their own companies as well as of the public that invested with them and bought their products. So much for Gramm's argument that "informed institutions tend to develop their own system of safeguards and protections." That very assumption that financial markets are inherently self-regulating was what enabled their ruin, and with it the refutation of the Reagan Revolution.

As I write this, I think of something Ronald Reagan would often tell me and other reporters who covered him: That he had an enduring respect for FDR. As early as 1964, when Reagan was first running for governor of California, he would explain his conversion from New Deal Democrat to Goldwater Republican by saying, "I didn't leave the Democratic Party. The party left me." He would then go on to pay tribute to Franklin Delano Roosevelt, as he had in his earlier autobiography, for programs that saved the Reagan family during the Great Depression, when his unemployed father was able to find work only at a New Deal agency. For years Reagan had remained committed to that memory of an activist government righting the wrongs of the market and ameliorating the rough swings of the business cycle.

During his time at GE, however, Reagan endorsed the viewpoint that what was good for Big Business was good for America. And why not, since GE, under pressure from an aggressive union, provided solid manufacturing jobs that supported a then-growing middle class? Later, though, the conglomerate, mirroring shifts in the American economy as a whole, increasingly became dependent on financial products rather than material ones, such as refrigerators. So it was, when the crash came in 2008, that GE was one of the biggest basket cases, its stock sinking like a dropped anchor primarily because of the failures of its GE Capital unit, which had grown to become almost half the company. By the spring of 2009, the historic company, the only original member of the Dow Jones Index still on that index today, had lost its AAA rating and faced a whopping $269-billion loss in its stock market share value.

General Electric, in fact, could be the textbook example for how short-term greed can serve executives while destroying a company's future. Founded during the Great Depression to help folks buy GE appliances, GE Capital safely provided credit for fifty years to up-and-coming consumers. In the 1980s, however, with GE being run by legendary high roller Jack Welsh, the company put growth above all else. GE Capital rapidly expanded its loan business into areas where it had scant knowledge, including credit card and property loans.

By 2007, as the financial world was beginning its downfall, GE Capital accounted for 55 percent of the company's total profit. When the market crashed, the company tanked and was only saved by more than $100 billion in government guarantees for its loans. Reagan's old company, his inspiration, had fallen victim to the excess of the unregulated market that he had so fervently extolled.

Nor would it be easy to bounce back because now the public and its political representatives were wary and demanding regulation. The *Economist* magazine in its March 19, 2009, issue pointed out that "GE Capital flourished as a member of the 'shadow banking' system of firms that offered myriad financial products without having to bear the regulatory burdens of banks. In [the] future, firms that perform bank-like activities can expect much stricter oversight, whether or not they have a banking license. That will impose greater costs on the business."

Regulation would come back by popular demand because of the pain imposed on the nation by unbridled corporate greed enabled by the very business deregulation that Reagan had sought. Getting government off the back of business, his red-meat campaign rally slogan, turned out to be disastrous for business.

The rub lies in the need for the modern corporation not to be left alone without adult supervision. As they say, it's good to have some locks in the house to keep the honest people honest. Government rules regarding product safety, humane working conditions, and proper internal accounting are in fact not only good for business but also essential for the modern corporation to function. That is particularly true in the financial services industry, where the rewards for chicanery are so dizzyingly enormous that relying on personal morality in the war between conscience and greed is a sure loser. Certainly that has been obvious in many of the recent corporate scandals, but there are still some who believe, despite the evidence to the contrary, that a completely unfettered free market is the way to go. Certainly, Reagan believed that, and his rhetoric about ending oppressive government regulation had a compelling impact for most of three decades. But the problem is that the deregulatory forces he unleashed eventually provided the annoying facts on the ground that demolished his grand expectations for the efficiency of fully self-regulated markets.

Ironically, the real economic legacy of what has been ballyhooed as the Reagan Revolution was to set the stage rhetorically for the unheralded yet dramatic changes that would come later, under Clinton. Long after Reagan had left Washington for his California ranch, the amazing power couple Phil and Wendy Gramm would fulfill his dream of destroying New Deal restraints on banks by enacting actual legislation to accomplish just that.

The Gramms would increase their power during the next four years after Reagan under the first President Bush, when she took over the CFTC and he rose to leadership on financial issues in the Senate. But the full measure of success, that of implementation of the deregulation of Wall Street sought by President Reagan, would only come in the second term of the Clinton era. In the end, it would be a bipartisan victory but on ideological terms that Reagan had defined.

CHAPTER 3

The
Clinton Bubble

What a difference a decade makes.

It's difficult to recall, after the banking meltdown, the mood during the Clinton years, when the call for radical deregulation of the financial industry was all the rage. Back in the late 1990s, there was widespread agreement among Wall Street lobbyists, leading politicians from both parties, and the business media that radical financial industry deregulation was—as one of its prophets, Senator Phil Gramm, would proclaim—"the wave of the future."

We had entered a brave new world of international computerized banking, and the high rollers on Wall Street insisted that laws regulating their activities were archaic and needed to be reversed. Fed chair and DC cult celebrity Alan Greenspan said regulations were unneeded anyway, because free markets were self-regulating. As Chapter 2 highlighted, perhaps the most important target of this mania was the granddaddy of New Deal banking legislation, the Glass-Steagall Act, designed to prevent another Great Depression and to rebuild trust in banks.

Glass-Steagall was designed to protect both the savings and the loans of average-Joe clients of commercial banks by shielding them from the gambling shenanigans of high-flying Wall Street investment banks such as J. P. Morgan and Lehman Brothers. A line was drawn: Either you were a bank that took deposits from, and made loans to, unsophisticated customers, or you were an investment house playing with rich folks' money in the stock market and even more risky markets; no longer could you be both.

Even with the anger at Wall Street prevalent during the Depression, passage of Glass-Steagall was extremely arduous, with the powerful banks aligned against it. However, congressional investigator Ferdinand Pecora looked into bank practices and uncovered risks for depositers that dramatically changed the terms of the debate. As economic historian Jill M. Hendrickson wrote in the October 2001 issue of the *American Journal of Economics and Sociology* of those pre–Glass-Steagall days:

Common practices uncovered by the investigation included the following: reputable investment houses that pushed on unsuspecting investors the securities of a company in which they were closely associated; speculation on the stock exchange; and evasion of income taxes on huge earnings by investment bankers. These questionable activities were aided by the commercial banks as they advised their depositors to use their affiliates' security salesmen for investment advice. The disclosure of these abuses through Senate hearings and the press shocked the public and paved the way for government regulation.

For six decades after the passage of Glass-Steagall, regulation had worked just fine. The American economy benefitted from the stability it imposed, with the world trusting its capital to the U.S. banking system. Runs on banks became a thing of the past, and the local bank loan officer became a trusted figure in the American neighborhood pantheon.

Not content to leave well enough alone, however, profit-hungry CEOs and shareholder boards, riding the merger and acquisitions craze of the 1980s and '90s, decided they needed to get bigger to fully control the market. The bank lobby had succeeded in chipping away at the regulatory barriers, particularly through rulings of the banking-dominated Federal Reserve, and emasculating regulatory agencies, but now they wanted the big prize: the repeal of storied Glass-Steagall.

Confidently forcing the issue, two major Wall Street firms led the way in attempting the mother of all mergers, in clear violation of the law. Either their merger would come apart over government-forced divestiture of profitable elements, or the law would have to change. They bet the bank, literally, on the latter, with every expectation of victory, given that the drive to repeal Glass-Steagall included not only Wall Street lobbyists but also the most influential news organizations. "A Monster Merger" was the headline of an April 8, 1998, *New York Times* editorial. It sounded like a criticism, but actually the editorial wildly celebrated the creation of Citigroup, the love child of the Citicorp-Travelers Group merger and in particular its architects, John Reed of Citicorp and Sanford Weill of Travelers, for forcing a "modernization" of the law:

> They have announced a $70 billion merger—the biggest in history—that would create the largest financial services company in the world, worth more than $140 billion. If regulators approve the merger, Citigroup, as the company will be called, will serve about 100 million customers in 100 countries. In one stroke, [they] will have temporarily demolished the increasingly unnecessary walls built during the De-

pression to separate commercial banks from investment banks and insurance companies.

Nor was there much evidence of that purported indelible line between the newspaper's editorial position and its journalistic coverage when it came to financial deregulation. A news story in the *Times* that same day echoed the editorial's theme, that the merger would force a reversal of the dreaded New Deal legislation. The lead paragraph of the story, ostensibly straight news reporting, gushed over this "bold merger," reading like a press release for Citigroup:

> In a single day, with a single bold merger, pending legislation in Congress to sweep away Depression-era restrictions on the financial services industry has been given a sudden, and unexpected, new chance of passage. Just a week ago the measure, the eleventh attempt in two decades to update the nation's banking laws, was written off as dead. But the announcement on Monday of a giant merger of Citicorp and Travelers Group, not only altered the financial landscape of banking, it also changed the political landscape in Washington.

As elsewhere in the mainstream media, the tone and emphasis of the article implied that everyone—consumers and bankers alike—would benefit from what proved to be a disastrous merger. The *Times* indicated no possible downside to this development in the innocuous-sounding "financial services industry." Note the use of the friendly word "update" in the *Times* article, rather than "repeal," "subvert," or even "betray."

The news story continued: "Indeed, within 24 hours of the deal's announcement, lobbyists for insurers, banks and Wall Street firms were huddling with Congressional banking committee staff members to fine-tune a measure that would update the 1933 Glass-Steagall Act separating commercial banking from Wall Street and insurance, to make it more politically acceptable to more members of Congress."

How could novelty-obsessed Americans not want something that was sixty-five years old replaced with something new and "fine-tuned"? This is not to pick on a single newspaper; other leading news organizations also served as cheerleaders for the new legislation. But the *Times*, as perhaps the nation's most respected news source, best illustrates the bias at work: What should have been shocking in the newspaper's recounting of Wall Street's manipulation of the legislative process was presented as the inevitable march of progress. The notion that what the lobbyists wanted might prove disastrous to the economic interests of the American people was rarely considered by the media.

The regulators at the Fed and elsewhere went along with the grand proposal, giving the new company a two-year waiver from compliance with Glass-Steagall. Thanks in part to Citigroup's lobbying and the enthusiasm of the media, Congress would replace Glass-Steagall entirely a year later.

The language of the *Times* editorial was typical of the mass media response in accepting the assumption that "modernization" meant giving Wall Street lobbyists what they wanted. Picking up on that semantic cue, the new law replacing Glass-Steagall would be called the Financial Services Modernization Act. A year later, another law was passed in the closing weeks of the Clinton administration guaranteeing not only the legality of the new conglomerates but also the dubious financial products that were at the center of their anticipated profit. That measure, which provided "legal certainty" for the over-the-counter derivatives that would cause the meltdown eight years later, was called the Commodity Futures Modernization Act.

Upon signing the first measure, President Clinton seemed giddy with excitement over just how modern all this was, even as it pushed aside key achievements of the most celebrated president—Franklin Delano Roosevelt—his party has ever produced. "Over the [past] seven years, we have tried to modernize the economy," enthused Clinton. "And today what we are doing is modernizing the financial services industry, tearing down those antiquated laws and granting banks significant new authority."

The president later presented one of the pens he used to sign the measure into law to a beaming Sanford Weill, who no doubt was pleased with the "legal certainty" the act granted his company and obviously not expecting the "significant new authority" granted to him and other bankers to lead to his bank's collapse within a decade. Weill would proudly mount the pen on his office wall.

"In the 1930s, at the trough of the Depression, when Glass-Steagall became law, it was believed that government was the answer," said a similarly exuberant Senator Phil Gramm, the bill's primary author, at the signing. "We are here today to repeal Glass-Steagall because we have learned that government is not the answer . . . I am proud to be here because this is an important bill. It is a deregulatory bill. I believe that this is the wave of the future."

Indeed it was, a future in which Gramm retired from the Senate to become a top executive with Swiss-based UBS, which subsequently suffered enormous losses in the banking meltdown and had to be bailed out by both the Swiss and the U.S. governments. It was also a future in which Enron, where his wife Wendy was a key member of the audit committee, would go belly up. A little government regulation might have benefitted those family-connected enterprises.

Gramm himself would be ignominiously dismissed as the key economic adviser to 2008 Republican presidential candidate John McCain after his comments denying the recession was real and blaming the collapse of the economy on its victims. As he put it in an interview with the *Washington Times*, Gramm said, "You've heard of mental depression; this is a mental recession . . . We have sort of become a nation of whiners. You just hear this constant whining, complaining about a loss of competitiveness, America in decline" despite economic growth.

One of those who did sound the alarm but was himself dismissed as a whiner back in the heyday of the deregulation frenzy was Democrat Byron Dorgan of North Dakota: "I think we will look back in ten years' time and say we should not have done this, but we did because we forgot the lessons of the past," said Dorgan, one of only eight senators to vote against the Financial Services Modernization Act. Ten years after the *New York Times* editorial celebrating the deregulation that Dorgan opposed, a financial columnist for the paper would write in a terrific understatement, "Today, a few years earlier than he predicted, Dorgan looks prescient."

The near-collapse of Citigroup came nine years and six months after the *Times* editorial confidently assured America that "Citigroup threatens no one because it would not dominate banking, securities, insurance or any other financial market."

The federal government, later concluding that the merger celebrated by the *Times* had produced a true monster "too big to fail," prevented its total collapse by pumping $50 billion directly into it, while also guaranteeing $300 billion of Citigroup's "toxic assets." Clearly, the merger of Citigroup had ended up a considerable threat to U.S. taxpayers and, indeed, to the entire world economy.

Clinton was dispossessed of the wisdom to foresee this disastrous outcome of the bills he signed into law, or else he simply fell under the thrall of Wall Street hucksters—or both. *Wall Street Journal* deputy Washington bureau chief Monica Langley, in her book *Tearing Down the Walls: How Sandy Weill Fought His Way to the Top of the Financial World . . . and Then Nearly Lost It All*, relates the following conversation between Weill and his new partner, John S. Reed, the head of Citibank, on the eve of their public announcement of the planned creation of the biggest private bank in the world:

> Sandy suddenly suggested, "We should call Clinton."
> "Who?" Reed asked.
> "The president!" Sandy replied. "Let's tell him about our merger."
> Reed was still puzzled. "Why?"

Langley recounts how Weill then explained to Reed that it would be possible to schedule a quick conference call with the president of the United States, regardless of the fact that it was a Sunday night. Within minutes Clinton was on the line. During the call Weill briefed the president on the merger that would be unveiled the next day. Then, "President Clinton told him about his recent trip to Africa . . . Reed assured the president that Citibank, which had a long presence in Africa, intended to increase investments in that region. After their ten-minute chat, Sandy hung up, crowing, 'We just made the president of the United States an insider.'"

That anecdote, presumably verified by the many interviews Langley conducted with Weill, Reed, and others involved, and never challenged by them, tells more about how the U.S. political economy actually functions than most college classes on the subject. Notice, for example, that there was no questioning by the president as to what effects the unprecedented merger—which would create the world's largest financial services corporation with 100 million customer accounts—would have on ordinary Americans and the overall economy. Nor was there any concern about the legality of this move, despite its clearly violating Glass-Steagall. But as Weill correctly observed, the president had become an insider, complicit through the phone conversation in validating first the merger and then the legislation that made it legal.

Later, a half-decade up the road, deregulation would increasingly come to be widely associated with revelations of usurious loan rates, shady subprime mortgages, and enabling the spectacular rise and fall of Enron. The new Citigroup, in fact, soon would be deeply involved in the financial shenanigans of the Enron debacle, ending up having to pay $2 billion to settle a lawsuit by the University of California pension fund and others alleging Citigroup engaged in defrauding investors.

By November 2009, Weill's original partner in the Citigroup merger, John Reed, would express regrets for the evisceration of Glass-Steagall: "I would compartmentalize the industry for the same reason you compartmentalize ships," he told Bloomberg. "If you have a leak, the leak doesn't spread and sink the whole vessel. So generally speaking, you'd have consumer banking separate from trading bonds and equity."

So much for the benefits of "modernization"—a semantic device critical in selling the freewheeling brave new world of financial manipulation through a compliant media echo box. Aside from William Safire's columns and a small number in a similar vein, including mine in the *Los Angeles Times*, a review of the contemporary media finds little in the way of serious discussion of possible objections to the legislation.

Safire, the *Times'* conservative columnist who had worked for Richard Nixon and was not normally considered a Ralph Nader type, nevertheless understood the threat of corporate power run amok. Among the few to sound the alarm, he raised his voice alongside that of Nader, pointing out that a major positive consequence of the New Deal regulations was that commercial banks had been prevented from gambling with depositors' savings, which were insured by the Federal Deposit Insurance Corporation, created by Glass-Steagall.

"No private enterprise should be allowed to think of itself as 'too big to fail,'" wrote Safire in a foreshadowing of exactly what would ensue. Having the support of the FDIC—the federal government guaranteeing your accounts—had to come with restrictions, or it would be exploited, he argued.

"Federal deposit insurance, protecting a bank's depositors, should not become a subsidy protecting the risks taken by non-banking affiliates. If a huge 'group' runs into trouble, it should take the bank down with it; no taxpayer bailouts should allow executives or stockholders to relax."

Nevertheless, a rapid victory by Citigroup's opportunistic supporters—other banks and free-market ideologues—had seemed at hand after the Clinton administration signaled it would beat back additional objections by privacy advocates, including Safire and some skeptics in Congress, led by liberal Representative Ed Markey and conservative Senator Richard Shelby. They had argued that allowing the merger of insurance companies, stockbrokerages, and commercial banks would destroy the privacy protection of customers when those databanks were combined.

Markey and Shelby were demanding that the law specify that no information could be shared unless consumers gave specific written permission for it to be shared, referred to as "opt-in." But the White House had backed the alternative favored by the financial institutions, "opt-out," under which information could automatically be shared unless the consumer notified the institution in writing *not* to do so. The clear message from Clinton was that he was fully allied with leading Republicans on the Senate and House banking committees, which had drafted the bill.

Even with such a seemingly unstoppable alliance, however, the new legislation's authors almost overreached. Senator

Phil Gramm, chair of the Senate Banking Committee and the main author of the Financial Services Modernization Act, otherwise known as the Gramm-Leach-Bliley Act, decided to gild the lily by going after one of his pet peeves: the Community Reinvestment Act (CRA). This was a package of laws that attempted to prevent mortgage lenders from redlining poorer and minority communities by forcing banks to make their loan approval process more transparent and accountable. When Gramm weakened such provisions in his new bill, his partnership with the Clinton White House was jeopardized by objections from liberal Democrats.

The revolt came at a moment when the fix was in and the Clinton administration was fully backing the congressional Republican leadership in giving Wall Street what it so desperately wanted. Despite the media cheerleading and, far more important, a $300-million financial services industry lobbying campaign and unprecedented campaign contributions, the "update" of Glass-Steagall ran into trouble. That was the message from Gramm to Citigroup's top lobbyist, who in response warned the senator to urge Citigroup's Weill to intervene aggressively, especially with his good friend Bill Clinton.

While apologists for the big banks since the meltdown often have questioned, with false naïveté, what changing the law had to do with the collapse of too-big-to-fail banks such as Citigroup, Weill leaves no doubt as to the importance of the repeal of Glass-Steagall in his memoir, *The Real Deal: My*

Life in Business and Philanthropy, which he wrote with Judah
S. Kraushaar. He also leaves no doubt that the support of the
Clinton administration was critical to that effort. During vis-
its with other industry leaders to Washington, "I developed
a particularly good relationship with Gene Sperling, President Clinton's point man on financial services reform, and
worked closely with him in devising our lobbying efforts. At
the same time, Merrill's [Merrill Lynch's David] Komansky
focused on setting up meetings with Bob Rubin, who in 1998
and early 1999 still ran the Treasury Department."

Sperling, whom Clinton had once referred to as the MVP
of his financial team, went on to become chief counsel to
Treasury Secretary Timothy Geithner in the Obama administration (after serving as a consultant for the long-running
TV political drama *The West Wing*). For those concerned
that too much is made here and elsewhere about the role
of the Clinton administration in moving toward radical
deregulation, Weill's account of how he got the act passed
is instructive.

Some Democrats during the 2008 presidential campaign,
including candidate Obama, would hit hard on the fact that
the act that replaced Glass-Steagall was primarily pushed
through by Republican free-market ideologue Phil Gramm,
who for a time was the chair of the John McCain campaign.
More abject Clinton apologists would add that support for
the bill was so strong, it was veto proof, implying that, although the president expressed enthusiasm for the bill upon

signing it, he had been of little consequence in its passage. That version, however, is sharply contradicted by Weill's own published account of events, which presents Gramm as more obstacle than asset.

Describing the significance of Gramm replacing "important political ally" Alfonse D'Amato, the then Republican senator from New York, as chair of the Senate Banking Committee, Weill complains that Gramm "appeared uninterested in serious reform and never missed a chance to remind me that there were no important banks, brokers, or insurance companies domiciled in his state of Texas. In other words, financial services companies were far from his natural constituency." Another problem was territorial rivalry between the Fed's Alan Greenspan and Treasury's Robert Rubin (who would later work for Weill at Citigroup) over which branch of government would wield what remained of regulatory power in the new paradigm.

"By early 1999, prospects for meaningful reform seemed to have dimmed considerably," Weill recalls in his book, noting that spats between the Federal Reserve and the Treasury Department over jurisdiction inhibited progress, as did particularly lethargic leadership in the Senate. With the 2000 election looming, Weill feared even lukewarm support for regulatory reform would evaporate, as few politicians would make the financial services industry a priority.

But just as things were looking hopeless, Rubin decided to retire and pass the torch of Treasury secretary to his deputy, Lawrence Summers, whom Weill credits with saving the day.

(Again, as with Sperling, we have an example of a Clinton alumnus who would go on to work for the Obama administration, in this case holding the very same job in the White House that Sperling had occupied as top economic adviser to the president. Like Sperling, Summers would also have no problem supporting Clinton camp rival Obama, indeed helping write the campaign speeches in which the candidate attacked the very legislation Summers had helped push into law.)

Weill remembers how Rubin's decision to resign thrilled him, as the choice of Larry Summers as a replacement "indicated a far more flexible stance versus the Fed." His excitement was not premature—members of Congress, particularly James Leach, chair of the House Banking and Financial Services Committee, and Commerce Committee head Thomas Bliley, quickly "lined up to support new legislation."

Still, the Clinton White House had a problem in coming through for Weill: As a devoted "triangulator," the president needed a face-saving device to deal with those on the more liberal side of the party in Congress who were worried about weakening the progressive Community Reinvestment Act. Weill was obliging, pulling what journalist Langley would call "his most important trump card" from his pocket: good friend, civil rights activist, and serial presidential candidate Jesse Jackson. That's a showstopper: Jesse Jackson, champion of the underdog, rides into town to save the day for the biggest concentration of financial power ever?

Just as both houses of Congress passed similar bills, set to sail through the conference committee and onto a willing president's desk, the CRA issue crystallized, and last-minute snags developed. According to Weill, "the Congressional Black Caucus expressed reservations about whether large financial institutions would serve the interests of the poor. When I learned about this concern, I decided to call Jesse Jackson and ask for his support."

It was a classic mutual back-scratching moment, and it was Jackson's turn to return some big favors to Weill. The bank executive described candidly in his memoir his relationship with the civil rights leader and how it came to work to his advantage.

> I had met Jesse several years before when he protested our deal with Shearson out of a mistaken fear that we'd cut services to low-income clients. At the time, I worked hard to allay his concerns and subsequently agreed to support his initiatives to promote minority employment on Wall Street and advance financial literacy training in poor neighborhoods. Jesse and I had since become good friends to the point where I felt comfortable asking for a return favor. Jesse Jackson came out publicly in support of the financial modernization bill, and his support proved timely and effective.

Langley's biography of Weill, while providing a fascinating behind-the-scenes perspective, shares the failing of her subjects in treating objections to the legislation by consumer and community activists as little more than annoying speed bumps on the road to "modernization"—the catch-word that ended up in both the title of this bill as well as its complementary legislation the following year, the Commodity Futures Modernization Act.

"The impasse threatened to kill the legislation that was vital to Citigroup's survival as the first American 'universal bank' in seventy years," the business journalist writes in the cheerleading style typical of her colleagues. Again, this is the myopic business journalism that plays down noneconomic controversy, indeed complexity, as a boring annoyance because it does not improve the bottom line.

The Weill-Jackson alliance is not as complicated as it is depressing, especially for longtime supporters and fans of the eloquent, passionate Jackson. Over the years since he famously stood on the balcony with Martin Luther King Jr. as King was assassinated, Jackson had developed a number of lucrative operations that depended on corporate contributions—and Weill was one of his big contributors.

It is not the place here to fully examine the motives of either man in forming this alliance, and they certainly offered much justification for their joint acts of "charity," which extended from support for the Harlem-based Alvin Ailey dance troupe to Jackson's Wall Street Project, aimed at getting more African Americans into important positions on Wall Street, where they were unquestionably underrepresented. According to Langley, Jackson had recruited Weill to be the project's first cochair. Perhaps Jackson saw Weill, who was born to modest means in Brooklyn, as sharing his civil rights aims.

Langley writes of Jackson, "The civil rights leader developed a mutually beneficial bond with Sandy, forged by their respective encounters with racism and anti-Semitism." No matter the basis of their collaboration, it worked out splendidly for both men. Jackson continued to receive lucrative contributions from Weill for his enterprises, and Weill achieved the moral beard as an "enlightened" capitalist. But Weill also got something more important to the bottom line: Jackson as a shill for the radical deregulation of the financial industry.

Of course, Jackson was not the only progressive to weigh in on banking deregulation. Its biggest critic was legendary citizen activist Ralph Nader, a DC veteran not easily snowed by anyone, including Jackson. Nader continued to sound the alarm, as did a host of community-based groups working against discrimination in housing. But what Jackson's endorsement of the bill accomplished was to provide the Clinton administration with cover, especially from members of the Congressional Black Caucus.

Thus, the trump card worked as Weill had intended. As he writes in his book *The Real Deal*: "Just as we were about to cross the goal line, one last obstacle arose. Senator Gramm, ever the savvy horse trader, took exception to a provision in the bill which forced banks to invest in poor areas . . . One afternoon he called and threatened, 'Call your friend Clinton and get him to change the provision or else I'll fire my rockets and blow your bill apart.'" Worried, Weill immediately called Gene Sperling, who was less than intimidated. Sperling laughed and explained that Clinton "wouldn't respond" to Gramm's threat.

Apparently Sperling didn't know how eager Clinton was to please Weill, who ended up being pleasantly surprised by the president's accommodation to Gramm's demand. "I thought the worst and assumed Gramm would follow up on his threat, but an hour passed and nothing happened," Weill writes. Gramm called again the following day, but, Weill adds, Clinton managed to mollify him. On November 12, the president signed the Gramm-Leach-Bliley Act into law, an accomplishment that in one "stroke modernized the structure of the financial services industry."

While Monica Langley's reportage basically accords with Weill's memory of those events, she supplies more detail as to how the last-minute deal went down. She notes, though does not seriously examine, the fact that the Clinton-Gramm compromise left the CRA protections "watered down," representing a betrayal by Clinton and Jackson of their often-proclaimed concern for the poor. Langley writes:

> Now Jackson came to the defense of his old friend. He met with Gramm privately to tell the committee chairman that he would support a watered-down version of

the community-reinvestment provisions, a move that would signal to other consumer groups that they should back off and let the legislation proceed. The only remaining hurdles were President Clinton and the Democratic members of the [Senate Banking] committee following his lead. On October 21, 1999, during a marathon negotiating session with the Democrats, Gramm couldn't persuade them to give sufficient ground. Furious, he stormed out of the committee meeting room and strode angrily over to Roger Levy, Citigroup's senior lobbyist.

"You get Sandy Weill on the phone right now," barked the senator, jabbing a finger into Levy's chest. "Tell him to call the White House and get them moving, or I'll kill the bill. You have one hour."

Langley reports that Weill then called the president, saying the bill was in trouble unless a compromise could be reached with the Democrats. She says that Gramm brought Hillary Clinton into the fray, telling the president, "If my wife were running for Senate in New York, I would not veto this bill."

Hours later, Gramm announced victory, and the bill would go on to become law when Bill Clinton signed it.

"The final hurdle to passage of the bill was the Community Reinvestment Act, which obligates banks to provide credit to citizens in minority and low-and moderate-income areas and which is the bête noire of Phil Gramm," the *Nation* magazine editorialized in its issue dated November 15, 1999, three days after the bill was signed into law. "Gramm did not succeed in obliterating the CRA, but with the Clinton Administration's acquiescence, he went a long way towards eviscerating it. Under the conference bill there will be no ongoing sanctions against holding company banks that fail to meet the CRA standards. And it will lessen the number of CRA examinations, making it harder for regulators to insure that banks are complying with their obligations to the poor."

Odd then, that when the deregulation of the Clinton years lessened the pressure on the banks to lend to poor people, Republicans after the banking meltdown of 2008 would attempt to blame the subprime mortgage mess on Democratic do-gooders forcing lenders to help out the underclass. In reality, the number of subprime mortgages previously had been steady and grew dramatically only after deregulation. The surge was not a consequence of increased pressure on the banks to make such loans; on the contrary, it was the desire to sell collateralized debt obligations, given "legal certainty" by deregulation that made shaky mortgages newly attractive to the banks.

Why? Because whereas commercial banks previously had held mortgage-based debt obligations, now they were offloading the long-term responsibility to others to either collect or foreclose on them. While some poor people certainly were eager to accept loans they would have trouble paying back, it was not their happiness the bank was worried about, but what would turn out to be a gushing profit well: the packaging of debt obligations as securities.

In the aftermath of the downfall of Citigroup—some parts of it dismembered and sold off while the rump remained a ward of the state—those Americans who wonder why their pensions and savings were wiped out might just reflect on a summation from Langley's biography of Weill. "President Clinton soon signed into law the Financial Services Modernization Act of 1999. Critics predicted a wave of mega-mergers, but the biggest one was now secure," she writes. "The legislation was soon tagged the 'Citigroup Authorization Act.'"

Weill's close ties to Clinton had paid off. It secured the future organizational structure of the company. As Weill notes in his book, he and Phil Gramm joked about the powerful bill years later, saying their law should have been called the "Weill-Gramm-Leach-Bliley Act."

"Pride goeth before destruction and a haughty spirit before a fall" seems a suitable proverb to quote here. The reality hit in 2001, the first year of the George W. Bush administration, when WorldCom, Enron, and other huge conglomerates enabled by deregulation began to implode. By 2005, seven years after its glowing editorial and news reports celebrating the overturn of Glass-Steagall, the *New York Times* had come back down to earth in its assessment of Citigroup and the other mergers permitted by that deregulation.

Even before the banking meltdown and at a time when Citigroup stock was still high, the *Times* ran a story on September 11, 2005, based on an exclusive interview with Weill as he was exiting from his leadership of the bank. The headline, "Laughing All the Way from the Bank," was ironic given that the paper itself, as with most of the business press, had been in on the joke from the beginning:

> Adorning a conference room wall on the third floor of Citigroup's Manhattan headquarters is an enormous wooden plaque. It bears a likeness of the company's chairman, Sanford I. Weill, and lists every deal he engineered to create what is now the country's largest, most profitable and most influential financial institution. The inscription beneath his image reads: "The Man Who Shattered Glass-Steagall." That is a reference to the Depression-era law that hemmed in the size and powers of America's banks for several decades, until the 1998 merger that formed Citigroup helped lead to its repeal, ushering in a new age of boundless, hazardous, high-octane finance and deal-making still struggling to sort itself out.

Just how hazardous to the world's economy would be revealed within the next few years, but in a sharp break with its past reporting, the *Times* in that story finally admitted to the dark side of the "Monster Merger" it had once lauded and to the cost of "updating" regulations that had worked well for six decades: "Glass-Steagall, the hoary law that Citigroup's creation helped to displace, was intended to prevent conflicts among consumer, commercial and investment banking. Yet Citigroup became a focal point of nearly every investigation that examined such conflicts, most notably in relation to its role in the collapses of WorldCom and Enron. The bank eventually paid more than $4.65 billion to settle regulatory inquiries and class action lawsuits." Quite a tribute, even if intended as backhanded, to that "hoary" law—a description suggesting regulation that had outlived its usefulness, rather than essential guardrails that should have been reinforced, not eliminated.

The merger mania represented by the formation of Citigroup was an effort to take advantage of synergies in the market, to merge the resources of the older established institutions with the ambitions of the high flyers. That was what the marriage of staid old Citibank and the various hustling companies that Weill had collected under his Travelers umbrella was all about. In that sense, by permitting such mergers the new law would allow a new culture of irresponsibility that Glass-Steagall had been designed to prevent.

The creation of a new financial permissiveness—the new law's main significance—was captured best by Nobel Prize winner Joseph E. Stiglitz, who as chair of Clinton's Council of Economic Advisers had attempted to oppose that and other deregulatory moves of the Greenspan-Rubin-Summers team but was unsuccessful. As he described the significance of the repeal in a January 2009 article in *Vanity Fair*:

> The most important consequence of the repeal of Glass-Steagall was indirect—it lay in the way repeal changed an entire culture. Commercial banks are not supposed to be high-risk ventures; they are supposed to manage other people's money very conservatively. It is with this understanding that the government agrees to pick up the tab should they fail. Investment banks, on the other hand, have traditionally managed rich people's money—people who can take bigger risks in order to get bigger returns. When repeal of Glass-Steagall brought investment and commercial banks together, the investment-bank culture came out on top. There was a demand for the kind of high returns that could be obtained only through high leverage and big risk taking.

That is exactly what the new Citigroup set out to do from its first year after the new law certified the enterprise's legitimacy. And where better to find those huge profits than in the new but rapidly expanding business of unregulated derivatives, led by the packaging of various forms of high-risk mortgage and other consumer credit accounts?

So the subprime meltdown begins not with concerned liberals in Congress attempting to put more poor people into homes they can afford, which is what the CRA was about, but rather those like Weill wanting to milk housing for the poor for all it was worth—home chattel to be packaged into securities and sold. Sandy Weill, for all of his appeal to Jesse Jackson and the editorial board of the *New York Times*, had a record before the Citigroup merger of being into such deals. After leaving his post as president of American Express, which had acquired Weill's brokerage firm, Shearson Loeb Rhoades, Weill got Control Data Corporation to spin off its ailing Commercial Credit company, and hand Weill the reins to take the company public. He later invested $7 million of his own money in the firm, became its CEO, and slashed costs to make it more profitable. He then engineered several mergers and acquisitions, the biggest prize being the huge insurance firm Travelers, of which Weill became chair and CEO.

After the merger of Travelers and Citigroup, Commercial Credit became CitiFinancial, specializing in subprime mortgage lending. Another unit of Citigroup, CitiMortgage, specialized in "A" paper lending, the alternative mortgages later so critical to the real estate meltdown. But not satisfied with already playing a leading role in the cheap exploitative credit market, Citigroup explored buying Countrywide and then settled on Associates First Capital, another leading subprime lender.

Associates was described at the time by the *Economist* magazine as a company whose three "most attractive" businesses are: "lending at high rates to low-income American borrowers; lending at extremely high rates to American credit-card borrowers; and lending at staggeringly high rates to Japanese borrowers."

This is the true face that Democrats, even some so-called liberal Democrats, brought to the mortgage crisis driven by pro-business toadying and hardly a surfeit of idealism. What Clinton did, in alliance with Republicans like Gramm, is open the floodgates for an unprecedented soaking of the poor. According to a true community conscious observer, Maude Hurd, who worked with the ACORN group, the acquisition by Citigroup of Associates was a marriage of two bad actors when it came to concern for the poorer communities that ACORN deals with. In a December 8, 2000, article in the *American Banker*, she wrote: "There are serious problems with Citigroup's failure to make good loans in low-and moderate-income communities and to minority borrowers. Associates has a notable record of outrageous predatory lending practices like manipulating and misleading borrowers so as to be able to charge exceptionally high interest rates and fees, and engaging in flipping and equity stripping are basic elements of their business, not occasional aberrations."

Mark those words, and be not fooled by the liberal pretensions of a Weill and the politicians who served him. This is the early smell of the subprime scandal in its birthing, as Hurd wrote: "The pattern of racially and economically bifurcated lending by prime and subprime lenders inevitably produces more expensive credit for minority and lower-income borrowers. Citigroup had been guilty of this in the past, and the purchase of Associates magnifies the problem manyfold."

The problem only got worse as Citigroup increased its holdings and expanded into the securitization of that bad debt. As late as the fall of 2007, when the mortgage business was already in trouble, Citigroup's response was not to get out early, as Goldman Sachs would, but to jump in deeper, acquiring other lenders who were in trouble with their bad paper and hoping to make another killing. "Citigroup's investment banking arm scooped up the assets of troubled subprime mortgage lender ACC Capital Holdings yesterday, the same day that the struggling company announced that it was closing," the *New York Times* reported on September 1, 2007. The story went on to note that with the acquisition "Citigroup bought up the remnants of ACC's Argent wholesale mortgage origination division as well as the servicing rights to collect on more than $45 billion in home loans."

There is more to the story of the meltdown; bad loans are a key part of it, but, as the next chapter discusses, the ability to package those bad loans as securities and then sell them in an unregulated market drastically compounded the problem. It is of more than symbolic interest that Citigroup, the one enterprise that most energetically and at considerable cost pushed for the end of Glass-Steagall, should end up being a ward of the state because of the culture of greed that Stiglitz warned against. It is also of note that Stiglitz's nemesis in the Clinton administration, Robert Rubin, would end up joining Citigroup, with compensation averaging $20 million a year while the company sowed the seeds of the great banking debacle.

But while Rubin had departed government for Citigroup, his former assistant, Lawrence Summers, took over at Treasury and, as we saw before, was instrumental in giving that final push for the passage of the FSMA. A year later, he would have an even more significant and ultimately disastrous legislative accomplishment with the passage of the Commodity Futures Modernization Act. That, for Wall Street sharks, was the blood in the water.

CHAPTER 4

The
Valiant Stand
of Brooksley Born

If an honest movie were to be made about the banking meltdown, it would be an upscale DC version of Julia Roberts's *Erin Brockovich*. The heroine whistleblower would be real-life regulator Brooksley Born, a Clinton appointee who took her job seriously enough—and had the experience and knowledge—to become a thorn in the side of elite executives and politicians who wanted to look the other way as long as the derivatives well was gushing cash. The villains would be a bipartisan cabal of Wall Street lobbyists and their shills in government, beginning with the team *Time* magazine dubbed the "Committee to Save the World"—Robert Rubin, Alan Greenspan, and Lawrence Summers. Born battled these financial behemoths for the mind and soul of Bill Clinton, and it was Born—and the public—who lost.

The plot would center on Born, head of the Commodity Futures Trading Commission (CFTC), having the gall to fulfill her public duty by trying to police all these newfangled financial gimmicks, unregulated derivatives of all sorts, which she believed, correctly, had enormous destructive potential. But she would slam into a wall erected by the nation's most powerful financial titans. There would be cameos by respected financier Warren Buffett, famously tagging these devices as "financial weapons of mass destruction," and Franklin Delano Roosevelt, whose prescience about needing to protect consumers was about to be fully betrayed.

Buffett, the most successful and celebrated investor in the land, would be scoffed at as an alarmist, making it no surprise that the much earlier moves by Born, a relatively unknown regulator pushing for more transparency in OTC commodity trading and greater oversight by her agency, were aggressively blocked.

Flashing forward, of course, we now know all too well that the giant over-the-counter system was a gambling den of big players betting on all manner of futures through these contrivances. But back in 1996, the year Born was appointed to head the CFTC after a quarter century of deregulation and nonenforcement of New Deal safeguards, this new regulator would begin her dramatic fight against a powerful outgoing tide.

To set the scene, the CFTC is an independent government agency claiming in its mission statement that it "assures the economic utility of the futures markets by encouraging their competitiveness and efficiency, protecting market participants against fraud, manipulation, and abusive trading practices, and by ensuring the financial integrity of the clearing process."

But when Born arrives to head the commission, it is an underpowered agency mainly monitoring the traditional agricultural commodity futures traded on established exchanges. Her predecessor Wendy Gramm stayed true to her ideological commitment to keep the financial derivatives markets unregulated even as those markets were beginning to spiral dangerously out of control. Born sees that new and unregulated futures markets are shooting up everywhere, from the online energy and metals dealings pioneered by Enron to the mortgage and credit card debt bundling aggressively undertaken by lenders old and new. Not long after taking the commission post, Born, a pioneering lawyer with considerable private practice experience in the business world, seeks to put out the derivatives fire before it spreads out of control. It is those efforts that are worthy of cinematic homage.

Born, who a decade later would begin to be seen as a modern-day Cassandra, recognized the problem immediately, as she would recall in a 2003 interview for *Washington Lawyer* magazine: "I became concerned about it once I got to the commission and began to learn about the OTC market. The more I learned, the more I realized we didn't know." She understood clearly that U.S. and international markets were facing great danger. She referred to Alan Greenspan himself, who said one of the reasons the Federal Reserve Board had supported the bailout of Long-Term Capital Management (a large hedge fund) was that they were "afraid it would have profound worldwide economic repercussions."

A *Wall Street Journal* article by Michael Schroeder and Greg Ip published December 13, 2001, five years after Born's appointment, explained the escalating tension: "[Born's] comments in speeches and in a discussion paper about the need for more oversight and regulation of OTC derivatives triggered an uproar among derivatives dealers—from J. P. Morgan to Enron. They quickly complained to Congress and other regulators that the uncertainty Ms. Born was creating could destabilize their markets."

This fear that the goose that laid the golden eggs might be killed was quickly making Born persona non grata in the corridors of power. In dramatic fashion, according to the *Wall Street Journal*, she was summoned in June 1998 from the hospital bed of her daughter, who had undergone knee surgery, by Representative James Leach, chair of the House Committee on Banking and Financial Services, to an emergency meeting in which "regulatory staff and lawmakers berated

Ms. Born for more than two hours in a fruitless effort to persuade her to stop her campaign."

Three months later, the collapse of Long-Term Capital Management led Leach to offer a grudging acknowledgment that Born wasn't crazy. "You are welcome to claim some vindication," he said at a congressional hearing.

Born was still alive and kicking. Yet she had already aroused the extreme hostility of an army of corporate advocates—especially the formidable DC lobbying machine of Enron, which was "fanatical about preventing any hint of derivatives regulation" according to the *Wall Street Journal* reporters' sources. Enron, however, donated primarily to Republican candidates and courted party heavyweights such as Wendy Gramm, by now a member of the company's board, and George W. Bush, who would later be embarrassed by his close connections to Enron's top dog, Ken Lay—"Kenny Boy," as the president affectionately nicknamed his friend. In the 2000 election, Enron would bequeath 72 percent of its $2.4 million in political donations to members of the GOP.

Born had been appointed by a Democratic president, however. Couldn't she tell Enron and the rest of her adversaries to back off? No. As it turned out, the Goliaths who would hammer this David of a regulator were much closer to Bill Clinton than to Enron, more New York than Texas.

Befitting our drama, they come straight out of central casting, as described in a four-thousand-word puff piece headlined "The Three Marketeers," in one of the nation's leading newsweeklies, *Time* magazine. The February 15, 1999, cover story, carrying the title, "The Committee to Save the World," fawns over Federal Reserve chair Alan Greenspan, Treasury secretary Robert Rubin, and his deputy and handpicked successor, Lawrence Summers, who are riding the crest of an economic boom and wielding power nothing short of comic-book awesome. They also have the ear and confidence of a self-proclaimed "reform-minded" president who by now has come to accept the destruction of his own appointee, Brooksley Born.

The three members of this particular boys' club are shown preening with smug self-confidence on *Time*'s glossy cover. They seem to bond over everything from playing tennis to setting interest rates. The *Time* story is an unabashed ode to their presumed brilliance. "Rubin, among others, says the joy of working with Greenspan lies in both the power of his intellect and the sweetness of his soul," the article reports.

"The quiet romance of the man [Greenspan] has always been present if you looked hard enough," gushes Joshua Cooper Ramo, then the magazine's foreign editor.

Timothy Geithner, who served under Rubin, says of his mentor that he ran the Treasury "more like an investment bank," though given the track record of some of them that might no longer be taken as a compliment.

The soul of the more prickly Summers is not described as sweet, but *Time* assures readers that his "intellect never fails to dazzle." The owner of this shining intellect was at that moment leading the troika in pushing Congress to prevent the regulation of derivatives but ten years later would admit that the instruments he had valued so highly were at the heart of the nation's financial collapse.

The derivatives controversy, Brooksley Born, and anything else that might intrude on the image of their collective decency and high intelligence are simply omitted from the *Time* story. The glowing takeout stands as an enormous embarrassment to the famed magazine's branded "access journalism": in its wanton praise of the three—who gave Ramo a great deal of what he called "private" time—the *Time* article is all too typical of the uncritical media coverage they had received until the banking meltdown.

"What holds them together is a passion for thinking and inextinguishable curiosity about a new economic order that is unfolding before them like an Alice in Wonderland," writes Ramo. "The sheer fascination of inventing a 21st century system motivates them more than the usual Washington drugs of power and money. In the past six years the three men have merged into a kind of brotherhood with an easy rapport."

That the brotherhood crushed all who got in its way, particularly a sister in the person of Brooksley Born, who got it right when the brothers got it wrong, is not mentioned. In America, everybody likes a winner, and, indeed, they would easily convince the president and Congress to fundamentally alter the financial markets through sweeping new deregulatory laws.

Their first great victory was the passage of the Financial Services Modernization Act in 1999. The second, and perhaps more important, effort was to get a law passed to prevent regulation of the burgeoning derivatives market. But before they could do that, they had to deal with Born, who refused to roll over like a typical ambitious Washington bureaucrat. It is amazing that she lasted as long as she did, facing such a stacked deck as she prodded and poked this barely comprehensible magic moneybox of OTC derivatives.

To understand why, one has to realize that she was not a pampered political appointee receiving a payback for fundraising but a tough, savvy expert with a track record of taking on unpopular fights as an underdog—and winning them. She also is a woman of annoyingly strong convictions who was known to possess a flaw fatal for the budding careerist: a moral center.

It was no surprise to those who knew Born that in her actions in government service, her empathy would reside more comfortably with the general public than with Wall Street heavyweights. Unlike many top government appointees, she was not a prep school product but rather a graduate of the public Lincoln High School in San Francisco. Her father headed the city Public Welfare Department, while her mother was a public school teacher and later a vice principal. As she told Narda Zacchino for a profile we co-authored for

Ms. magazine: "They believed that we all had a responsibility to contribute to our society and particularly those of us who were lucky enough to get a good education and have supportive parents should have a special obligation to do public service work."

In the mid-1950s, at age sixteen, she landed at Stanford, forty-five minutes down the San Francisco Peninsula. There, after taking tests (blue for male students, pink for female—she took both) to assess career interests, she was steered away from a doctor's career by a counselor who, upon learning that being a physician appealed to Born whereas nursing did not, told the young woman that wanting to be a doctor and not a nurse indicated she was more interested in making money than in caring for people.

Such outdated gender ideas were still common in the 1950s, of course, and Born soon realized she was not going to achieve much if she continued to listen to such naysayers. So, armed with what she later recalled for *Washington Lawyer* as a "ferocious sense of injustice," and urged on by her mother, she entered Stanford Law School, where she would become the first female editor of the *Stanford Law Review*, a prestigious honor for which she was nationally recognized.

To understand how Born years later could go toe-to-toe with the intimidating old boys' network of Greenspan, Rubin, and Summers, one must realize that she had been doing that sort of thing her entire life. She became an attorney at a time when only 3 percent of the country's lawyers were women. She entered Stanford Law in a class of 155 men and 10 women—only 4 of whom would graduate from this bastion of testosterone three years later, in 1961.

Born was not a quitter. Nor was she a political neophyte. After working for a law firm that represented unions and clerking for famed Washington, DC, appellate judge Henry Edgerton, she accepted an offer from the Arnold & Porter firm, both because it had defended politically unpopular clients, including some persecuted by Senator Joseph Mc-Carthy, and because it had hired and promoted many women. While developing a successful career as a corporate lawyer, Born also played a leading role in changing the profession's treatment of women.

Born cofounded the National Women's Law Center and continues to serve as chair of its board, was a founder of the Women's Legal Defense Fund in 1971, worked within the American Bar Association as chair of the Individual Rights Section, founded the ABA women's caucus, urged ABA support for the Equal Rights Amendment and Title IX of the Education Amendments, and worked to get women into decision-making positions in the ABA. She also was the first woman to serve on the ABA panel that evaluates federal judicial candidates, including Supreme Court nominees.

As Born reached the pinnacle of her legal career, she became so highly regarded that her name ended up on the short list for attorney general of the United States when Clinton became president. Although he eventually chose Janet

Reno instead, in his next term he made Born head of the CFTC because of her credibility in the practice of business law. The irony is that while Born would come to be dismissed by her male counterparts in the Clinton administration as naïve about finance, she actually had far more experience in the law concerning derivative trading than her male critics collectively possessed. As she recounted in the *Ms.* interview:

> I had been representing foreign entities, including foreign banks for a while, probably in the early 1970s in my practice . . . and in the mid '70s, the London Futures Exchanges came to the firm and needed representation because the United States had just set up the Commodity Futures Trading Commission and had just decided for the first time that the federal government would regulate not just trading in domestic agricultural products like wheat and pork bellies but also in financial instruments and international commodities like energy products, metal products, international agricultural products like coffee, sugar and cocoa.
>
> And the new commission was not very sophisticated about the international markets that it was in effect now regulating the US activities in, and so the London Exchanges retained us to work before the CFTC to kind of help explain the international markets and also to make sure that the regulation that was

> being adopted here wasn't impacting, having an ad-
> verse impact in London. So I began to practice before
> the CFTC and also to take cases in the courts involving
> derivatives issues and eventually became the head of
> the firm's practice in the area as it grew.

(One of her cases was a highly publicized one involving the infamous cornering of the silver market by the billion-aire Hunt brothers.)

The CFTC is overshadowed by the larger regulators, especially the Securities and Exchange Commission, and Born could have simply kept her head down and not rocked the boat in her first public service job. Instead, this Lone Ranger among financial industry regulators focused like a laser on the underregulated OTC derivatives, which had been legally permitted for the first time just two years before by then-CFTC chair Wendy Gramm.

This allowed the business to expand to $100 trillion annually, Born said in the *Washington Lawyer* interview. "Alan Greenspan," she continued, "said that the growth of this market was the most significant development in the financial markets of the 1990s. The market was virtually unregulated and many, many times as big as the trading on the futures exchanges."

She noted that the CFTC "had kept some nominal authority over this market, but there were no mechanisms for enforcing the rules. For example, antifraud rules were retained, but no reporting was required. The market was completely opaque."

Born grew more concerned that no federal regulators knew what was going on in the OTC derivatives market, no one seemed to know how it worked, and serious problems—the near collapse of Bearings Bank and Long-Term Capital Management, which had $1.25 trillion worth of derivatives contracts with less than $4 billion in capital to support them—were not triggering any red flags of warning. She told *Washington Lawyer* that as she was looking into OTC derivatives, she believed the market "was a nightmare waiting to happen" and that "some federal regulator should have information *before* a disaster occurred rather than only afterward."

As a result, Born decided to issue a "concept release" document seeking input from the industry and other interested parties concerning the need for more oversight and transparency of the market. As happens when any group of people sense a threat to their skyrocketing profit margins, those trading in this market created a firestorm of criticism, attacking the idea and its author. They were joined by strange bedfellows—other financial regulators.

To Born, the response was shocking. As she said in the *Ms.* interview, "I was absolutely mystified that both the industry and the other financial regulators did not even want to ask questions about an enormous financial market that none of us had any insight into. And it concerned me gravely that the market was so fragile that people felt questions could not be asked about it."

Inside the White House, Born's peers on the President's Working Group on Financial Markets responded to her questions as if she were the enemy of a boom they were claiming credit for having created, rather than showing gratitude for her due diligence in regulating the futures market.

Alan Greenspan, SEC chair Arthur Levitt, and Robert Rubin had all discouraged inquiry into these issues, encouraging Congress to pass legislation that would prohibit the commission from taking any regulatory steps on OTC derivatives, Born told *Washington Lawyer*. There were no hearings, but during a "congressional conference committee meeting on an appropriations bill, an amendment was added preventing the commission from taking any action on over-the-counter derivatives for six months. This occurred within a month after Long-Term Capital Management's collapse!"

In addition to Born, the President's Working Group on Financial Markets included Summers, Greenspan, Rubin, New York Federal Reserve president Bill McDonough, Levitt, and other financial regulatory chiefs. In his book *In an Uncertain World*, Rubin wrote that "some members of this group thought that derivatives . . . by their nature could pose a systemic risk." That statement was a surprise to Born.

"Not anyone in that group indicated to me that they shared my concerns about systemic risk," she said in the *Ms.* interview. "Some might have secretly shared them and not said anything, and certainly some didn't share them and said a lot."

There is plenty of evidence of the latter. Michael Greenberger, a former director of the CFTC's trading and markets division, recalled in an interview with public television's *Frontline*: "I walk into Brooksley's office one day; the blood has drained from her face. She's hanging up the telephone; she says to me: 'That was Larry Summers. He says, "You're going to cause the worst financial crisis since the end of World War II"'; that he has, my memory is, thirteen bankers in his office who informed him of this. [He told her,] 'Stop, right away. No more' . . . It was not done in a tactful way, I'm quite confident of that."

The *Wall Street Journal* in a retrospective story on December 13, 2001, reported that extraordinary pressure had been put on Born to back off. Enron lawyer Ken Raisler, himself a former CFTC general counsel, met with CFTC commissioner John E. Tull Jr. to complain about Born's activities. Tull, previously a supporter of Born, then turned around and, "according to people with knowledge of the meeting," informed her he was "withdrawing his support at Treasury's request."

This synergy of action between the Clinton White House and Enron, which the *Wall Street Journal* reported was "fanatical about preventing any hint of derivatives regulation," plays against the close link between Enron and the Republicans. The fact was that neither political party was interested in anybody looking too closely at a key engine for a profit bubble that was making the investor class very, very happy.

In the 2003 *Washington Lawyer* interview, Born is diplomatic in looking back at the passage of the 2000 law. "I thought it was very bad policy, but on the other hand it was Congress's decision to make, and having made that decision, Congress relieved the commission of its responsibility, so that Enron, for example, became the Congress's responsibility, not the commission's," she said.

Michael Greenberger was more blunt, blaming Congress for giving derivatives dealers a "blank check to operate 'opaque and nontransparent to the government as a whole,'" according to the *Wall Street Journal*. "You don't know the leverage of these things," Greenberger said. "They're playing with fire."

Fire, indeed. And after ignoring glaring warning signs like the Long-Term Capital Management collapse, those at the top who told regulators to look the other way would bear grave responsibility when the baffling derivatives casino would eventually break the global economy.

The reality was that even those in government charged with monitoring these markets had difficulty following what was going on. Arthur Levitt, after his ten-year tenure as chair of the SEC, would admit that he had seriously underestimated the danger the derivatives market posed to the larger economy.

Federal Reserve chair Alan Greenspan, however, a free-market purist with unparalleled influence over economic policy, kept insisting the derivatives market would regulate itself. Greenspan, commonly called "The Oracle," in deference to the esteem accorded him by politicians and the media, as well as to his superconfident style, was an intimidating figure.

"I always felt that the titans of our legislature didn't want to reveal their own inability to understand some of the concepts that Mr. Greenspan was setting forth," Levitt recalled for the *New York Times* as the disaster unfolded in October 2008. "I don't recall anyone ever saying, 'What do you mean by that, Alan?'"

One of the rare Congress members who did, as the *Times* noted, was Representative Edward J. Markey, a Massachusetts Democrat who has been one of the most effective consumer advocates in Congress. In 1992, before Born's arrival at the CFTC, Markey sounded the alarm on unregulated derivatives from his perch as chair of the House subcommittee on telecommunications and finance. Markey requested a study on the subject by the General Accounting Office, as Congress's investigative arm was then known. When it arrived two years later, it clearly identified "significant gaps and weaknesses" in the government's regulation of derivatives.

At that time, in 1994, GAO leader Charles A. Bowsher in testimony before Markey's committee warned of the potential danger of a liquidity crunch from a fall in the derivatives market—precisely what happened fourteen years later with the abrupt collapse of giant firms like Lehman Brothers, Bear Stearns, AIG, and Citigroup.

"The sudden failure or abrupt withdrawal from trading of any of these large US dealers could cause liquidity problems in the markets and could also pose risks to others, including federally insured banks and the financial system as a whole," said Bowsher, as reported in the *New York Times*. "In some cases intervention has and could result in financial bailout paid for or guaranteed by taxpayers."

But none of that seemed to worry Greenspan, who assured Markey's committee that "risks in financial markets, including derivatives markets, are being regulated by private parties. There is nothing involved in federal regulation per se which makes it superior to market regulation."

With that prejudice serving as DC's Conventional Wisdom—capitalism will regulate itself, the Great Depression be damned—the government's role in the management of the economy came to be defined as extremely limited. In the playground of the lobbyists—the hallways and conference rooms of Congress—killjoys like Born were unwelcome.

The mass media, especially what passes for a business press in this country, went along, both because of a natural pro-corporate bias and because the subject was so dry and complicated and hardly reader- or viewer-friendly. Moreover, Greenspan and Rubin, in particular, had built up enormous reserves of loyalty and goodwill among the power elite, journalists included, and the media-shy Born had not, nor was her small agency well known outside a coterie of market experts.

Obviously, Brooksley Born was no newbie when she entered public service; her résumé alone spoke to her extensive knowledge of the derivatives markets, and her lifetime of trailblazing to secure rights for others made her extremely well prepared for a job protecting the public's interest in matters in which she was an expert.

But expertise, courage, and strong convictions can only get you so far in the brutal world of DC. As a pragmatist, she was not prepared for how ideological her superiors and rivals would turn out to be. She found out soon enough, however, when she was called to The Oracle's lair: Alan Greenspan's private dining room at the stately headquarters of the Federal Reserve.

Rick Schmitt reported the encounter with the living legend, as recalled by Born, in an article for *Stanford Magazine*: "'Well, Brooksley, I guess you and I will never agree about fraud,' Greenspan told Born, mysteriously. 'What is there not to agree on?' Born replied. 'Well, you probably will always believe there should be laws against fraud, and I don't think there is any need for a law against fraud.' Greenspan, Born says, believed the market would take care of itself, needing no regulation."

Of course he did, being a lifelong devotee of the radical free-market ideology of writer Ayn Rand. So it was opportunistic for Clinton—ostensibly a Democrat who believed, as he often insisted, in the role of progressive government—to turn over the government's most powerful tool in managing the economy to someone who didn't believe in government. The president placed his faith in the free-market extremism of Greenspan, and the Wall Street–first approach of Rubin and Summers, because he believed they could deliver rapid growth.

"Clinton made a deal with Greenspan in the first year of his administration that if the Fed kept interest rates low, the president would reciprocate with financial market deregulation," Robert Reich, who served in the Clinton cabinet as Labor secretary, told me in October 2009. He added that it was the deal that Rubin engineered and that defined the economic policy for the Clinton White House, to Reich's deep dismay.

In the end, it is clear that Rubin, Summers, and Greenspan were the key players, and they operated from a narrow ideological stance as true believers.

Bizarrely, the *Time* magazine piece on the trio describes this "faith" as "pragmatism," in an awkward attempt to reconcile their alleged genius with a simplistic perspective that ignored any evidence—the Great Depression, say—that would undermine it:

> The three men have a mania for analysis that has bred a rigorous, unique intellectual honesty . . . Their faith is in the markets and in their own ability to analyze them . . . This pragmatism is a faith that recalls nothing so much as the objectivist philosophy of the nov-

elist and social critic Ayn Rand [*The Fountainhead*, *Atlas Shrugged*], which Greenspan has studied intently. During long nights at Rand's apartment and through her articles and letters, Greenspan found in objectivism a sense that markets are an expression of the deepest truths about human nature and that they will be ultimately correct . . . That imposes a limit on how much they will permit ideology to intrude on their actions.

Adherence to an ideology as a defense against the influence of ideology seems an odd claim, but it allowed the three officials to preempt any naysayers—be they Arthur Laffer, the supply-side theorist of the Reagan era, or truly pragmatic regulators like Born—who were worried about the potential consequences of market turmoil. In this way, honest debate was short-circuited.

In retrospect, "history already has shown that Greenspan was wrong about virtually everything, and Brooksley was right," law professor and former investment banker Frank Partnoy told *Stanford Magazine* in a 2009 article. "I think she has been entirely vindicated . . . If there is one person we should have listened to, it was Brooksley."

Whether out of ignorance or expedience, however, Clinton approved of a campaign to shoot the messenger. The first bullet fired was a letter to congressional leaders signed by Rubin, Greenspan, and the SEC's Levitt that, as the *Washington Post* reported, "asked Congress to immediately pass legislation imposing a moratorium on the derivatives study launched by Born 'to protect this market from unnecessary and potentially damaging legal uncertainty' that might cause derivatives users to transfer their business offshore."

In other words, they were worried that if we looked too carefully at how the sausage was being made, its producers might freak out and move their abattoir to the Caymans. This was, no doubt about it, a sledgehammer response. Here were three members of the President's Working Group on Financial Markets asking Congress to stop a study—not legislation—suggested by Born, the group's fourth member.

The *Post* reported the response of Born's commission, which had not even seen the letter. "Born did not propose imposing regulations on derivatives when she announced her agency's study last month," a CFTC's spokesman noted. "She said that in the five years since the government decided not to regulate derivatives, the market has expanded so much that a new review of the risks is needed."

Summers, who would take over from Rubin as the head of Treasury the following year, successfully presented the case for a "see no evil" policy on derivatives before the Senate Agriculture Committee on July 30, 1998.

"As you know, Mr. Chairman, the CFTC's recent concept release has been a matter of great concern, not merely to Treasury, but to all those with an interest in the OTC derivatives market," Summers said. "In our view, the Release has cast the shadow of regulatory uncertainty over an otherwise thriving market—raising risks for the stability and competitiveness of American derivative trading. We believe it is quite important that the doubts be eliminated."

Why? Because, according to Summers, the unregulated derivatives market, which barely existed a decade earlier, was now assumed to be a key engine driving American prosperity.

"Mr. Chairman, the American OTC derivatives market is second to none," continued Summers. "In a few short years it has assumed a major role in our own economy and become a magnet for derivative business from around the world. The dramatic development of this market has occurred on the basis of complex and fragile legal and legislative understandings—understandings which the CFTC release put into question."

In other words, let the big boys play; this doesn't concern you. Of course, Summers expressed it a bit more elegantly:

> First, the parties to these kinds of contracts are largely sophisticated financial institutions that would appear to be eminently capable of protecting themselves from fraud and counterparty insolvencies and most of which are already subject to basic safety and soundness regulation under existing banking and securities laws.
>
> Second, given the nature of the underlying assets involved—namely supplies of financial exchange and

> other financial instruments—there would seem to be
> little scope for market manipulation of the kind seen
> in traditional agricultural commodities, the supply of
> which is inherently limited and changeable.

How hollow that assurance sounds a decade later, when Summers himself, born again as the top economic adviser to President Barack Obama, would help draft a proposal to Congress calling for the regulation of those same financial derivatives because there had been so much "market manipulation." Manipulation conducted by "sophisticated financial institutions" like AIG and Citigroup, whose top executives now admit they hadn't a clue about what their most aggressive derivatives traders were doing.

Born had known all along, but her warnings were consistently ignored, even as she refused to back down. The *Wall Street Journal*'s Michael Schroeder captured the hostility of Rubin and other Born critics in a November 3, 1998, article entitled "CFTC Chief Refuses to Take Back Seat in Derivatives Debate." The newspaper reported: "The nation's top financial regulators wish that Brooksley Born would just shut up. For nearly a year, Ms. Born . . . has been warning about the risk of unregulated over-the-counter derivatives."

Greenspan, Rubin, Summers, and Leavitt opposed Born's efforts to seek regulation, warning that threats of oversight could destabilize the financial markets and could also lead to lawsuits. Born's warnings continued to fall on deaf ears, the *Journal* reported, until September's near collapse of Long-Term Capital Management LP, the hedge fund whose "huge exposure to derivatives threatened to rock already-shaky world financial markets. Suddenly, the maverick CFTC chairwoman looked less like a turf-conscious alarmist and more like a modern Cassandra."

Cassandra or not, she was finished. Born's term was coming to an end, the president had never uttered a word of support, and she did not request a new term. Despite the startling evidence provided by the LTCM collapse, nobody at the top wanted to hear her dire warnings. Clinton himself must be held accountable for this one; by embracing the Republican deregulation mania and ignoring Born's prescient caution, he made a misstep far more damaging to the country than his dalliance with a White House intern.

A month after the LTCM bailout, Congress acceded to the pending request to ban any new regulations on over-the-counter derivatives for six months, which exceeded Born's term of office. A year later it would be made permanent, with the passage of the Commodity Futures Modernization Act (CFMA) in 2000.

A dazed preholiday Congress hurriedly passed the CFMA, despite its enormous implications for the future of the economy. Representative James Leach and Senator Phil Gramm, coauthors of the Financial Services Modernization Act (FSMA), which preceded it, pushed it through as an add-on to an omnibus appropriations bill one day before Congress adjourned for Christmas. There was no debate in the Senate on the amendment's merits, and the overall appropriations bill sailed through, for to oppose it would have meant taking money from Medicare, education, and the budgets of other popular programs. Lame-duck president Bill Clinton then signed it into law.

Although its passage was rushed, the bill had been years in the making, largely created as a response to Born's modest suggestions for regulation. But with her proposals for reform still being drafted at the CFTC even after she had left, the legislation was clearly designed to stifle any reform efforts.

Born had testified against an earlier version of the bill when it was still in committee, arguing that it "would prevent the Commission from taking action in market or other emergencies arising in that portion of the OTC derivatives market within its statutory authority" and "would for the first time eliminate the independence of the Commission as a regulatory agency by subjecting its actions relating to the OTC derivatives market to prior approval by the Secretary of the Treasury."

In other words, the only regulatory agency that understood derivatives was being told to back off and warned it had better ask for permission from the White House if it had any notion of not doing so. The legislation also successfully divorced the granters of subprime mortgage loans from any obligation to ever collect on them.

Finally, the bill's authors put in a blatant loophole in case anybody missed the overall message: "No provision of the

Commodity Exchange Act shall apply to, and the Commodity Futures Trading Commission shall not exercise regulatory authority with respect to, an identified banking product which had not been commonly offered, entered into, or provided in the United States by any bank on or before December 5, 2000."

Greenspan's fantasy had come true; the government was washing its hands of financial regulation. From here on out, the banks could do whatever they wanted. In less than a decade they would cannibalize themselves in an accelerated rush of high-stakes gambling, destroying $14 trillion of the wealth of American families in one seven-quarter period from 2007 through the first quarter of 2009.

After the '08 crash, as Born refused interview requests and carefully restrained herself from saying "I told you so," former SEC chair Arthur Levitt would be the only one of those who had blocked her reforms to admit he'd erred in not accepting her views.

"All tragedies in life are preceded by warnings," Levitt told *Newsweek*'s Michael Hirsh for a December 24, 2008, article. "We had a warning, it was from Brooksley Born. We didn't listen to that . . . I think that the explosive growth of a product that was unlisted and unregulated should have occasioned greater reaction."

Born probably was pleased with Levitt's admission, but surely she was less happy to find her old nemesis, Lawrence Summers, reappearing on the national stage as President Obama's top economic adviser. With consummate gall,

Summers, along with Rubin, was again posing as the solution to economic problems he had such a hand in creating. And without his head exploding and with a straight face, Summers under President Obama was now pointing to the passage of the CFMA as a major cause of the crisis.

When Obama made his June 2009 proposal for renewed regulation of the financial markets, it contained a detailed condemnation of the CFMA because it "explicitly exempted OTC derivatives, to a large extent, from regulation by the Commodity Futures Trading Commission. In addition, the law limited the SEC's authority to regulate certain types of OTC derivatives."

"As a result, the market for OTC derivatives has largely gone unregulated," the White House statement continued. "The downside of this lax regulatory regime for OTC derivatives—and, in particular, for credit default swaps (CDS)—became disastrously clear during the recent financial crisis."

Now they tell us.

In a *Washington Post* op-ed, Summers and Obama Treasury secretary Timothy Geithner, a Rubin/Summers protégé in Clinton's Treasury Department, bemoaned how "the most severe financial crisis since the Great Depression" was caused because the market "failed to perform its function as a reducer and distributor of risk. Instead, it magnified risks, precipitating an economic contraction that has hurt families and businesses around the world."

There was not a word of explicit self-criticism on the part of the duo that had done so much to help create this mess, both in the Clinton Treasury Department and afterward, when Geithner ran the New York Fed. Nevertheless, though it wasn't apologetic, the piece did concede enough to count as a damning rejection of their previous "pragmatism" on self-regulating markets.

"This current financial crisis . . . had its roots in the global imbalance in saving and consumption, in the widespread use of poorly understood financial instruments, in shortsighted-ness and excessive leverage at financial institutions," they wrote. "But it was also the product of basic failures in financial supervision and regulation . . . In recent years, the pace of innovation in the financial sector has outstripped the pace of regulatory modernization, leaving entire markets and market participants largely unregulated."

Incredible: This was exactly the straightforward and rea-sonable point Brooksley Born had been making a decade ear-lier when she was slapped down by Summers, Rubin, and Greenspan.

CHAPTER 5

They Have
No Shame

It was called the "Enron loophole." And without that pro-vision in the Commodity Futures Modernization Act (CFMA), the exponential growth and startling collapse of that notorious company would not have occurred. Some-times, corporate lobbyists should be careful what they wish for.

As a *Los Angeles Times* journalist covering the corporate deregulation battles of the past two decades, I found that congressional representatives or their staffers would often respond to my questions by helpfully referring me to lobby-ists who they conceded knew a great deal more about the subject than those actually paid by taxpayers to represent the public interest. That these staffers could do so without embarrassment speaks enormously to the incestuous arrangements of our political process.

Not only are these lobbyists seen as "experts" on Capitol Hill, rather than simply corporate mercenaries using cash to buy laws and access, but they are treated with a palpable respect, as are the corporate executives who often accompany them into the offices of the nation's senators and representatives. This makes more sense when one remembers that the bureaucrats and politicians inside the federal government are so frequently future lobbyists and corporate influence peddlers themselves; best not to get too high and mighty.

Whichever client they represent, be it a foreign dictatorship or mountaintop mining outfit, Microsoft or McDonald's, they are received as admired insiders, a resource to be milked for knowledge and campaign contributions. Their presence unchallenged and unquestioned, they tromp up and down the halls of power, writing laws, killing bills, and generally putting the lie to the fantasy of a government "of the *people*, by the *people*, for the *people*."

There is no clearer example of this blandly corrupt process than the infamous saga of Enron, the Texas firm that used political manipulation to make an Icarus-like crash-and-burn journey that would jeopardize the economy of the nation's most important state along the way. The passage of the CFMA, with its Enron loophole, is a particularly egregious example of how Enron influenced government policy, but this was not a one-off investment in the purchase of political credits.

While the scope and brazenness of Enron's shenanigans would become legendary, it is important to understand that the company did not stand in isolation. In fact, the story of Enron's lobbying is critical to explaining the meltdown of the entire world economy a decade later, since the legislation Enron executives so aggressively fought to pass also provided the "legal certainty" for the over-the-counter derivatives market that has come to haunt us.

As a consolation prize for an aggrieved public—from Californians to pensioners—the rapid implosion of Enron, and the subsequent lawsuits and congressional investigations, did allow a rare light to be trained on the otherwise opaque machinations of how corporations choreograph our democratic process.

Longtime Enron CEO Ken Lay, who later would profess grand ignorance of the practices of the company he headed, first saw from the inside how profitable it could be to game the political system as a prelude to gaming the energy market. He had been an economist in the Pentagon while a young naval officer and later undersecretary for energy of the U.S. Department of the Interior in the Nixon administration, where he worked on regulatory issues. Lay became convinced that the then relatively small company of Enron that he had taken over could become a money machine if it used the predictable earnings from its old-fashioned business of physically enabling the production and transport of energy to plunge into the wild and woolly business of energy trading.

Lay, who had moved Enron from backwater Omaha to the boomtown of Houston, was always focused on the politics. Perhaps his smartest play was to assiduously court the political super-couple of Wendy and Phil Gramm during the Reagan and first Bush presidencies; as chair of the Commodity Futures Trading Commission (CFTC), Wendy Gramm conveniently exempted Enron from key regulatory restraints and cleared the way for the first phase of the company's rapid rise toward energy market domination. Apparently unconcerned by appearances, she resigned from the CFTC in 1992 six days after granting the exemption—incoming President Bill Clinton would have certainly replaced her anyway—and a mere five weeks later accepted a position on Enron's board.

At the time, her husband was a recipient of significant campaign contributions from Enron, which reportedly paid Mrs. Gramm between $915,000 and $1.85 million in salary, attendance fees, stock option sales, and dividends from 1993 to 2001, according to the nonprofit consumer advocacy organization Public Citizen.

As the *New York Times* would report much later, this was a predictable pattern for Enron, and Wendy Gramm was not the first government official who was a recipient of the firm's largesse.

"Last year, as Congress and the Clinton administration debated whether to exercise more oversight of the financial instruments used by Enron and other companies to trade energy contracts, Mr. Lay courted Linda Robertson, a senior Treasury official who was the department's liaison with Congress," wrote the *Times'* Joseph Kahn and Jeff Gerth on December 4, 2001. "Ms. Robertson twice accepted paid trips to talk with company executives while she was still employed at the Treasury, her financial disclosure shows. The measure that became law, the Commodity Futures Modernization Act of 2000, specifically exempted energy trading from the regulatory scrutiny applied to brokers of money, securities and commodities."

That provision of the 2000 law contained the aforementioned Enron loophole that permitted the company to go hog wild in expanding its online electricity trading operation, ultimately leading to increasingly manipulative trading practices that would infamously lead to humiliating, life-threatening, and economically damaging rolling blackouts for California.

Robertson left the administration just weeks prior to the passage of the CFMA to become the top Washington lobbyist for Enron—a position she kept until the company declared bankruptcy at the end of 2001, a victim of its greed. Despite this blatantly apparent conflict of interest, in early summer 2009, Federal Reserve chair Ben Bernanke hired Robertson as a lobbyist as he sought to protect the Fed from congressional efforts to increase oversight of the secretive and monolithic central bank.

A few months later, Congressman Alan Grayson, a Florida Democrat, criticized her qualifications for that role, saying, "Here I am the only member of Congress who actually worked as an economist, and this lobbyist, this K Street whore, is trying to teach me about economics." K Street in Washington is the location of many lobbying firms. He later apologized amid an outcry of criticism over his language. There was no similar outcry over Robertson's selling her services to Enron.

When Enron did collapse, filing for bankruptcy on December 2, 2001, its market value shrinking in mere months from $77 billion to $500 million and its massive accounting fraud at the company exposed, deregulation critic Congressman Edward Markey (D-MA) would point out the larger lesson that easily could be missed in the company's sordid and colorful demise. "Enron is the sequel to California, it's all part of the one-year story line," he told the *Times*. "We can't leave energy products in the regulatory shadows. It hurts both investors and consumers."

This was a sentiment echoed by Michael Greenberger, one of the unsung heroes of the derivatives scandal, who had served as director of trading and markets at the CFTC under then-chair Brooksley Born. "Enron was getting very heavily into derivatives, and along with Wall Street banks, they went to bat to keep us away," recalled Greenberger in the *Times* story. Born, as described previously, had struggled valiantly to get the Clinton administration to recognize the huge dangers in the unregulated derivatives market and was crushed for her efforts by, among others, Treasury Secretary Lawrence Summers, who was Robertson's boss and strong supporter.

The best account of Enron's lobbying effort on behalf of the Commodity Futures Modernization Act was written by Michael Schroeder and Greg Ip of the *Wall Street Journal*, but unfortunately, this devastating report was filed only after the new law had begun creating its swath of economic destruction, bringing down greedy Enron and its huge and respected accounting firm, Arthur Andersen, which also went belly up almost overnight.

"A year ago, when most of the political world was obsessed with the deadlocked presidential election, Enron Corp. was quietly but aggressively lobbying Congress," the *Journal* reporters wrote in the December 13, 2001, article: "Its object: a little-noticed bill shaping federal policy toward the complex financial instruments known as over-the-counter derivatives."

Like Citigroup and other giant firms allied in the effort, Enron was correct that the already-booming OTC market would turn into an absolute gold mine if the CFMA could be passed. After two decades of currying favor with politicians from both parties, the firm's clout was mind-boggling. As the *Wall Street Journal* reported, Enron lobbyists actually were able to write specific language into the bill.

The company lobbied hard, and it paid off—the *Journal* reported that staffers of one congressional committee asked a lobbyist for an Enron-led industry group to "negotiate major aspects of the bill directly with regulators." The result of this was that Enron literally inserted certain measures into the bill that outlawed federal regulation of some of its flagship products, like "energy and metals derivatives, and its Enron Online energy-trading network."

Unfortunately, no such story was published in "real time," as the dirty work was being done. It was only the cratering of Enron—the company *Fortune* magazine had named "America's Most Innovative Company" for six consecutive years—that apparently led the business media to devote resources to describing how this piece of legislative sausage had been produced.

Considering the media and government attention Enron had manufactured before its fall, how was it that nobody was paying enough attention earlier to see the signs of disaster? "That's at least partly because Enron—as much as any company in America—had invested a lot of time and money over the past decade in keeping government out of its business," wrote Schroeder and Ip, in their retrospective.

As just a taste of those efforts, consider that in the year before Enron got its sweetheart bill passed, the company not only maintained a huge lobbying operation based in a twenty-eight-person Washington office—soon to welcome former assistant treasury secretary Robertson—it additionally doled out $2.1 million to other lobbying firms to aid in the work, according to the authoritative Center for Responsive Politics. These outside lobbyists and consultants included former Christian Coalition leader Ralph Reed; Michael Lewan, former chief of staff to Senator Joseph Lieberman; and Clinton's general counsel and Vice President Al Gore's former chief of staff, Jack Quinn.

Enron had an even larger contingent of Republican heavy-weights on its influence-peddling slate, including James Baker III, the first President Bush's secretary of state. Quinn teamed up with Ed Gillespie, former chair of the Republican National Committee, in 2000 to form Quinn Gillespie, a firm that earned $700,000 from Enron in 2001 alone to lobby the White House on the electricity crisis on the West Coast, according to the watchdog group Public Citizen.

Of course, in addition to the lobbying, millions were poured into the political campaign coffers. The company's donations favored Republicans by a ratio of three to one, according to disclosure records. Still, while much has been made of Lay's close ties to the Bush family—and I added to that chorus in my syndicated columns—Lay arguably received more payoff from his courting of the rival party, and court he did, donating $900,000 to Democratic candidates during Clinton's presidency.

"The fact is, Lay and Enron were working Washington long before George W. Bush came to town, and there was plenty of money and influence being spread around both political parties," reported the *Chicago Tribune* on January 13, 2002. "Lay . . . was no stranger to the Clinton White House, playing golf with the president and staying overnight in the Lincoln Bedroom."

Golf and sleepovers were nice, but Enron executives were not shy about making it clear that they expected dividends in this pay-to-play system.

"Enron made a $100,000 contribution in 1997 to the Democratic National Committee just days before it got to accompany Commerce Secretary Mickey Kantor to Bosnia and Croatia on a trade mission to the former Yugoslavia, where Enron hoped to win a large contract," the *Tribune* noted.

Regarding that trip, the *Boston Globe*'s Walter V. Robinson wrote on February 12, 1997, in an article headlined "Donations Are Linked to Kantor Trade Missions," that "with Kantor's help in Croatia, Enron signed a memorandum of understanding to construct a 150-megawatt power plant that will cost $100 million or more to build." The article noted the $100,000 contribution was made "whether by coincidence or gratitude" on July 5, 1996, six days before Enron's president took the trip.

There were other trade missions in which Enron executives accompanied Clinton administration officials to countries where Enron was trying to make multimillion-dollar deals. In fact, *Fort Worth Star-Telegram* reporters Jack Douglas Jr. and Jennifer Autrey, in a story on January 27, 2002, wrote that "Enron officials were so often part of Clinton's international trade missions that the company felt compelled to issue a news release saying no one from Enron was involved when a plane crashed in Croatia in 1996, killing all aboard, including Commerce Secretary Ron Brown." Kantor succeeded Brown in the cabinet post.

The *Boston Globe* article noted:

> During his nine-month tenure at Commerce, Kantor led only two small trade missions abroad. But an analysis done for *The Boston Globe* found that four of the companies invited, including Enron, gave the Democratic Party one-shot contributions of $100,000 or more just before or after the trips . . . Kantor said he was "stunned" to learn of the donations. He insisted that the trips and the contributions were entirely unrelated. Still, Kantor acknowledged that the size and timing of the contributions are likely to leave the public convinced that a quid pro quo was involved.

The public might also have perceived a connection between the $100,000 contribution and the Clinton administration's help in developing a multibillion-dollar project in India, one of several for which Enron got help from the administration. As *Time* magazine's Michael Weisskopf reported on September 1, 1997, Thomas "Mack" McLarty, Clinton's former chief of staff, provided assistance to businessmen who ponied up $1.5 million for the Democrats in the last election:

> On November 22, 1995 . . . Clinton scrawled an FYI note to McLarty, enclosing a newspaper article on Enron Corp. and the vicissitudes of its $3 billion power-plant project in India. McLarty then reached out to Enron's chairman, Ken Lay, and over the next nine months closely monitored the project with the US ambassador to New Delhi, keeping Lay informed of the administration's efforts, according to White House documents reviewed by TIME. In June 1996, four days before India granted final approval to Enron's project, Lay's company gave $100,000 to the president's party. Enron denies that its gift was repayment for Clinton's attention, and White House special counsel Lanny Davis says McLarty acted out of concern for a major US investment overseas.

McLarty later became a paid adviser to Enron.

All in all, the Center for Responsive Politics estimates 71 senators and 188 members of the House received contributions from Ken Lay or others at Enron. Individual Enron executives, especially Lay, also would donate and fundraise enormous sums for favored candidates; no opportunity to gain political capital was ignored. Enron and its employees gave President George W. Bush $736,800 in political and related contributions, serving, according to a Congressional committee report, as his number one political patron.

Despite the company's strong ties to the second President Bush—who later would most likely regret having given "Kenny Boy" Lay a nickname and calling his top fundraiser a "close friend"—it was quite eager to reward Robertson, who had served under Democratic Treasury secretaries Lawrence Summers, Robert Rubin, and Lloyd Bentsen, for her service on the Commodity Futures Modernization Act.

Robertson certainly wasn't perturbed by Lay or Enron's GOP bias: "This is an extremely dynamic, important company that has business in multiple arenas in which I've worked in the past," she gushed upon accepting the job. No kidding!

Enron's former vice president for corporate communications, Mark Palmer, did find himself fending off criticism from the political right over hiring a Democrat for its top lobbying job. He cited, accurately, "her experience" as a deciding factor and said that her "tool kit perfectly matched" what Enron was after.

Robertson became head of Enron's Washington lobbying office a month before the CFMA won congressional approval and President Clinton's signature in his last weeks in office. Robertson, who only weeks previously had been representing the administration in last-minute negotiations, was now there doing the same for Enron.

She was still dealing with the bill's primary author, Senator Phil Gramm, but now she was on the same paid team as his Enron-director wife, Wendy. Predictably, Enron had been a major contributor to Banking Committee chair Gramm's campaigns. Yet this super-alliance was only successful because it was in accord with the Clinton administration, which also supported deregulating OTC derivatives, including those involving energy.

The internal e-mails and other documents made public in 2001 after Enron's stunning fall from grace provide a rare window into just how this bipartisan jockeying on behalf of corporate interests works in the real world. As an example, consider this e-mail, sent by Enron lobbyist Chris Long to new colleague Robertson and other Enron lobbyists on December 12, 2000. (The "swap exemption" in the e-mail is a reference to trading on the future price fluctuations of a commodity—in Enron's case, energy. And while it is easy to understand that Enron didn't want regulators peering too closely into its deals, why would the Clinton Treasury Department, by then headed by Lawrence Summers, favor making it easier for the company to avoid scrutiny on "anti-fraud and anti-manipulation" of prices that so adversely affected consumers—as we would learn later from the California blackouts?)

> Treasury just minutes ago sent this compromise language to the CEA [Commodity Exchange Act] bill to Gramm's staff. It is my understanding from Treasury that the swap exemption is expanded slightly to say

that if you are trading on a facility (MTF) and you are
trading on principle-to-principle basis among eligible
contract participants you are no longer subject to anti-
fraud and anti-manipulation as contained in Sec. 107
of the House-passed legislation. This would be good
for us. Ken [Lay] is in London, so we can take a quick
look at the attached language and tell me if you con-
cur. Also, we need to take a look at the new Sec. 4 to
see if it causes any problems. They may cut a deal as
early as this afternoon!

That paragraph should be studied in high school civics
courses when they deal with that old staple lesson, "How a
bill becomes a law." Look at the dangerous synergy between
Lay, who would later be convicted of ten counts of securities
fraud and related charges, the Treasury Department under
a Democratic president, and a Republican senator whose
wife is on the Enron board, all pulling off something "good"
for Enron, a celebrated company that within a year would
be exposed as little more than a gambling front built on gaming markets and cooking the books.

Three days after that e-mail boasting of the progress in
the Treasury Department negotiations, Congress approved
the CFMA with the pro-Enron provisions included. The next
day an e-mail from Enron lobbyist Long to a list that included Linda Robertson and the company's top brass, led by
Lay and Jeff Skilling, celebrated the bill's passage, which

would "eliminate unnecessary regulation of commodity futures exchanges" and "open the door for Enron's further product innovation and growth."

In a subsequent e-mail Long was not shy about boasting that "Enron was a leading advocate of passage of this legislation. [CFMA was] over six years in the making and the collective support of many Enron employees has been crucial."

The law would indeed "open the door" for new products—including the sanctioning of securitized subprime mortgage packages at the heart of the economic meltdown seven years later—but unfortunately this proved fatal not only for Enron but nearly so for the economy as a whole.

Later, July 7, 2008, amid the wreck of the derivatives bubble, the nonpartisan Congressional Research Service published a report, "The Enron Loophole," to explain how the dodge had worked:

> Before its collapse in 2001, Enron Corp. was a pioneer in OTC trading and developed an electronic market (Enron Online) for trading physical and derivative contracts based on a number of energy products. Since the passage of the CFMA in 2000, an exchange-like market for energy derivatives has come into being. Trading occurs on electronic platforms among eligible commercial entities. Under the CFMA, the [Commodity Futures Trading Commission] had no substantive regulatory authority over these electronic trading facilities.

As the government watchdog nonprofit Public Citizen reported, the effect on Enron's bottom line was huge and immediate: "Because of Enron's new, unregulated power auction, the company's 'Wholesale Services' revenues quadrupled—from $12 billion in the first quarter of 2000 to $48.4 billion in the first quarter of 2001."

Ironically, another pioneer of deregulation—the state of California—would suffer a boomerang effect for its efforts in an embarrassing series of events that would bring unwanted national scrutiny to the house of cards on which Enron was built. Before the federal CFMA, it was perennially cutting-edge California that had bought into Enron's plan to liberate energy markets from the unwanted binds of government scrutiny and rules—supposedly a win-win for consumers and corporations alike.

Instead, it was a disaster for the state and the consumers because Enron was both big and brutal enough to game the market just opened up to it, in order to drive prices sky-high. One technique was to take power plants offline, famously exposed by audiotapes and transcripts released in mid-2004 by a small public utility near Seattle. The Snohomish County Public Utility District obtained thousands of hours of audiotapes along with hundreds of financial documents in its legal battle with Enron. The evidence, widely reported in the news media nationwide, revealed that Enron bilked consumers in the western United States of more than $1 billion.

The tapes are filled with obscene language and light banter as the energy giant's employees conjure ways to rake in millions of dollars for Enron in excess fees, in many cases literally leaving ratepayers in the dark during forced blackouts. In one of the taped conversations recorded four years before being exposed, an Enron employee identified as Enron trader Bill Williams III calls a Las Vegas Enron employee named "Rich."

> Bill: I'm giving you a call, ah, we've got some issues
> for tomorrow. You ready for some issues?

Rich says he will be on duty for a few more hours and that he has a pen and paper ready.

> Bill: . . . This is going to be a word-of-mouth kind of
> thing . . . we want you guys to get a little cre-
> ative . . . and come up with a reason to go down . . .
> Anything you want to do over there? Any . . . clean-
> ing, anything like that?
> Rich: Yeah, yeah, there's some stuff we could be
> doing.

The two agree that the power plant would shut down energy service to California for several hours, which would be during a peak energy demand, for "maintenance." Bill instructs Rich what to say to California utility officials. Rich consents but double-checks what he is going to be doing.

Rich: O.K., so we're just coming down for some
    maintenance, like a forced outage type of thing?
Bill: Right.
Rich: And that's cool.
Bill: Hopefully.

Both men laugh. They discuss a new written schedule Rich just received, which Bill says is "the one you're gonna want to ignore." Then he thanks Rich.

Bill: . . . I knew I could count on you . . .
Rich: No problem. I'm sure I'll have a good time. All
    right, so I've got you covered for tomorrow.
Bill: Thanks a lot Rich.
Rich: All right. I won't even put that in the book.

The next day the power plant was taken offline, forcing California to employ rolling blackouts to manage the emergency, which affected up to a half million consumers, according to the western power grid's daily logs.

A Snohomish County PUD press release detailed more of the taped transcripts:

Enron employees talked openly about "stealing" up to $2 million a day from California during the energy crisis. Traders also joke about taking money from "Grandma Millie" and making "buckets of money" from over-scheduling electricity transmission lines and taking power plants off line.

Related financial documents, covering the period of January 2000 through mid-2001, showed Enron manipulated energy markets on 88% of the days the PUD tracked. In one "ricochet" scheme, Enron illegally obtained $222,678 in a three-hour period by purchasing power in California, shipping it to Oregon where its original source was masked, and then reselling it into the California market for $750 per megawatt-hour. The scheme allowed Enron to avoid price caps.

Before California deregulated the energy trading market, only one "Stage 3" rolling blackout had been declared from June through December 2000; after passage, the state would suffer thirty-eight such blackouts, before federal regulators reluctantly intervened in June 2001.

Under massive public pressure, some senators, especially the two California Democrats, began demanding increased regulation, but the Bush administration would have none of it.

This was underscored in one of the e-mails, made public by congressional investigators, sent by Wendy Gramm and summarizing the trajectory of her influence. Now working for Enron, and dealing with a new Republican administration settling in after winning *Bush v. Gore* at the Supreme Court,

Gramm was eager to influence the structure of the one regulatory agency that had been questioning the exponential growth in derivatives markets.

The thoughts she expressed, particularly her hostility to regulator Brooksley Born and others at the CTFC who had taken seriously their mandate to protect the public interest, were intended for private communication with Steven J. Kean, Enron's former executive vice president and chief of staff. They provide rare insight into the mindset of those determined to prevent effective regulation.

Gramm is blunt in her adherence to ideological purity tests for all appointees to the CFTC—the folks running the regulatory agency must be unabashedly antiregulation. So it explains why she expressed a desire to unseat the commission's chair, James E. Newsome, because even though he "appears to be very free market," he was making moves that might actually lead to the enforcement of those few regulations left.

> From: WGramm@aol.com 02/14/2001 07:58 AM
> To: Steven.J.Kean@enron.com
> cc:
> Subject: Re: Confidential—CFTC Chair
>
> Hi Steve,
>   Folks love Newsome, and I think he's very nice and appears to be very free market. Spears, the other

Republican appointee is not at all free market, in my view. I would not like this to [be] mentioned anywhere else, but I have found that the farm reps on the Commission may sound deregulatory but are not, and have been really troublesome without a good free market person on board. And there are no truly free market persons on board at the Commission (every single other agricultural rep that I worked with on the Commission were trouble, even though they claimed to be deregulatory—and they were far worse before I got there and after I left.)

I visited with Newsome a day before Inauguration, and I was appalled at what they were planning to do concerning agency structure—that would have elevated the regulatory lawyers and diminished the role of the economists at the agency. Misguided and showed to me a lack of understanding of how organizational structures can affect what comes out of an agency . . .

The CFTC is in awful shape—the quality of staff is horrendous, and the Commission is relying on some of the worst people for their policy work (same folks that Brooksley Born used, same folks who have advocated more regulation of the OTC market for years). Many quality folks do not want the job as Chairman because it's been such a backwater. I am looking for some good folks. Have at least one person who would

be good at that job. And it's not Newsome. Please do
not share this information with the usual folks, as they
hate me anyway (I'm too free market and have argued
against their "fixes"). Sorry for this scathing review,
but this is an important appointment.

Wendy

In the end, Gramm was not able to get Newsome removed, perhaps a sign of the rapid wane of Enron's influence as the company's stock soured under a barrage of
negative press and revelations. Gramm herself was in hot
water. She was one of six members of the Enron Board's
Audit Committee and, according to the company's SEC filings, was "an overseer of Enron's financial reporting, internal controls, and compliance processes." The company's
mounting accounting scandals opened her to public criticism
and lawsuits.

Linda Robertson, too, was put on the run by Enron's
death spiral. After she landed on her feet as a vice president
of government, community, and public affairs at Johns Hop-
kins University, her official university biography managed to
omit that she had worked for Enron the two years prior. Was
this a rare moment of shame on her part or simply the behest of the respected university? She need not have been concerned, for her role as an Enron lobbyist did not prevent her
from finding employment later as a lobbyist for the Fed
when the Democrats came to power.

It is typical of Washington politics that largely the same cast of power brokers appears at every turn, protecting each other and their corporate paymasters inside the Beltway bubble. Even the exchange of political power, so dramatic at the end of a national election, is like a storm blowing waves on the ocean's surface while not far below everything is the same.

Thus, as Clinton passed the torch to Bush, the coddling of Enron continued against all odds and significant public pressure. Bush stymied California in its attempts to stop the company's abuses, perhaps happy with the bonus of seeing Democratic governor Gray Davis weak and embarrassed. Critics of Bush were particularly exercised about a private meeting in April 2001 between Lay and Vice President Dick Cheney that was instrumental in the drafting of the administration's energy policy, which—surprise!—ended up favoring Enron.

At that time, in early 2001, the California crisis was severe. Blackouts were affecting hundreds of thousands of angry residents; in March 2001 blackouts shut down electricity for 1.5 million Californians, and the giant Pacific Gas & Electric Company filed for bankruptcy. California officials seemed powerless to do anything and wanted government intervention in the form of price caps on wholesale energy sales to stabilize the wildly fluctuating energy prices. This would not have boded well for Enron, which was enjoying huge profits at California's expense.

As John Nichols reported in the *Nation* in March 2002, "even some Republicans were saying that caps made sense. But the caps would cost Enron—which had come to dominate energy markets by taking advantage of deregulation—a fortune."

Nichols noted that a very concerned Ken Lay arranged a meeting with Dick Cheney, "a man who had headed a corporation with extensive business ties to Enron and who had been a prime recipient of Enron's political largesse." The vice president "cleared his calendar" for the private meeting with Lay on April 17, "regarding what aides described as 'energy policy matters' and 'the energy crisis in California,'" Nichols wrote. "At the meeting Lay handed Cheney a memo that read in part: 'The administration should reject any attempt to re-regulate wholesale power markets by adopting price caps . . . ' The day after he met with Lay, Cheney gave a rare phone interview to the *Los Angeles Times* that had one recurrent theme: Price caps were out of the question. Dismissing the strategy as 'short-term political relief for politicians,' Cheney bluntly declared, 'I don't see that as a possibility.'"

A report prepared for Representative Henry Waxman (D-CA) by the then minority staff of the Committee on Oversight and Government Reform, which seemed to be pinning the entire Enron fiasco on the Republicans, makes much of this meeting. Yet such attempts seem a bit desperate when we find in the report that veteran Democratic Party player Linda Robertson was at the meeting as well, in her new role as Enron's top lobbyist. In fact, in the list of forty known contacts between Enron and the Bush administration that Waxman's staff compiled, she was present at eight of them.

If these meetings were so uniquely corrupt, why would Robertson be brought back into the government once the Democratic Party reclaimed the White House?

The report also seems one-sided in how it treats Enron's desperate end-game lobbying to stave off complete disaster. Ever reliant on government help, the company's new president, Greg Whalley, "called Treasury Undersecretary Peter Fisher six or eight times to ask the government to urge bankers to extend credit to the struggling company."

Sounds bad, and it was. Why should the U.S. government be intervening to help Enron? Yet what the report fails to note is that a Democratic icon, former Clinton Treasury secretary Robert Rubin, actually called Fisher as well, for a similar reason.

Rubin by now was securely ensconced in his executive position at Citigroup, a major creditor of Enron, which was going down fast. Rubin saw a chance to save this sinking ship, and he went for it, suggesting that Fisher intervene with credit agencies that were about to downgrade Enron's credit rating to gain more time for the banks to bail out the energy giant. In his memoir, written with Jacob Weisberg, he understates, "I prefaced our conversation by saying that my suggestion was 'probably a bad idea.'"

Rubin's role in this incident will be described in further detail in the next chapter; in short, Fisher did not make the call and reported it to his superiors, and, as Rubin feared, Enron sank. So he knew it was "a bad idea," yet Rubin contacted Fisher, risked damage to his own reputation, and amazingly wrote that he would do it again:

> Of course, in the wake of Enron's implosion and the stunning revelations of fraud and misconduct that followed, it became obvious that the company couldn't have been salvaged. I can see why that call might be questioned, but I would make it again, under those circumstances and knowing what I knew at the time. There was an important public policy concern about the energy markets—not just a parochial concern about Citigroup's exposure—and I felt that if a modest intervention by Treasury could potentially make the difference in avoiding a significant economic shock for the country it was worth raising the idea with an official there.

Fisher turned down Rubin's request, obviously agreeing with Rubin that it was not a good move to ask the Treasury official for this favor. So why did he make the call to suggest it? Was it at the instigation of Robertson, whom Rubin describes in his book as having been "our extraordinarily effective congressional liaison" when she worked for him at Treasury?

Let's assume not. Why look for dark conspiracy theories when the known facts of conflict of interest, outrageous betrayal of the public interest, and wanton sacrifice of integrity for blind ambition are so out in the open. A conspiracy is not needed when there is such a widespread assumption of common purpose and values that bind our elites, irrespective of whether they happen to be Democrats or Republicans or have taken another swing through the revolving door between public service and private profit.

Questions of integrity don't easily arise, for these people have evidently developed, as an essential condition of their success, immunity to shame.

★ ★ ★   CHAPTER 6   ★ ★ ★

Robert Rubin Rakes It In at Citigroup

The solid gold revolving door is, as the name implies, a particularly lucrative career passage between the highest halls of public and corporate power. In Robert Rubin's case, the door was platinum.

Few if any in American history have profited from their time in government as directly and immediately as President Clinton's Treasury secretary, yet a sycophantic press never saw anything untoward in Rubin's cashing in so shamelessly—at least until it could no longer ignore his role in the destruction of our economy.

In fact, Rubin was depicted frequently as something of a martyr in his service to the nation under President Clinton. Profiles emphasized this former chair of Goldman Sachs— where he previously earned mega-millions—commuting to New York to see his wife and making do for six and a half years with an expensive suite at Washington's landmark Jefferson Hotel, where he reportedly dined almost every night. And of course he was part of *Time*'s so-called Committee to Save the World.

So it was that when Rubin jumped directly from Treasury secretary to a $15-million-a-year job at Citigroup—a conglomerate made legal thanks to Rubin's deregulatory efforts—he received what amounted to a free pass for such a shameless money grab. Who could blame him, right? After his time slumming in the political trenches and indulging his liberal and civic instincts, went the story line, Rubin had been released to return to the challenging and exciting world of high finance from whence he came.

That work, in a "consigliere" position created especially for him, was described by Rubin and others as a challenge to his skills and intellect—the *New York Times* on November 23, 2008, said he was Citi's "resident sage"—rather than simply an opportunity to amass even greater wealth. Rubin's own 2003 memoir endorses this view. Four years after leaving the White House to be a top player at what was then the world's biggest financial services company, he described his new job as a learning opportunity and creative challenge rather than as a platform for plunder.

"Working in the financial sector would also give me an opportunity to stay current, to have the knowledge and insight that come from being engaged," Rubin wrote in his memoir. "That would help provide a basis for my involvement with the public policy issues I cared about and make my efforts to contribute to them more valuable."

While he does allow that he is "a reasonably commercial person" who wanted to do "something that would be financially rewarding," he does not acknowledge that jumping from Treasury to a spot just below CEO of the world's biggest financial services company could be perceived as a payoff for services rendered. (Rubin would earn more than $115 million at Citigroup before leaving the wrecked company in early 2009.) Even if he were a saint, wouldn't he want to explain how he avoided abusing such an obvious conflict of interest? And if not Rubin himself, how could those who gave the book such flattering reviews manage to so blithely ignore the obligation to at least rationalize it?

Similarly ignored is that the massive and historic banking deregulation that occurred on his watch made the conglomerate's existence legal and seemed designed to directly multiply Citigroup's profitability. While it did ensure the corporation's early profits, the new law also ensured its ultimate downfall, when Citigroup gagged on its surfeit of toxic derivatives, although that day of reckoning came five years after the memoir's publication.

As noted earlier, creating the largest financial conglomerate in the world from the stock-swap merger of Citibank and

Travelers Insurance depended on two key pieces of legislation approved during the Clinton years at Rubin's urging. The first was the Financial Services Modernization Act (FSMA), which gutted the historic Glass-Steagall Act and allowed Citigroup to become a sprawling leviathan—so giant that in the fall of 2008 it was deemed too big to fail by a federal government that rushed to guarantee its more than $300 billion in so-called toxic assets—and the second was the Commodity Futures Modernization Act (CFMA), which explicitly prevented the kind of regulation that could have saved Citigroup from the shortsighted avarice of its executives and directors.

Although Rubin was already ensconced at Citigroup when the CFMA was signed into law, he pushed for the legislation when he was Treasury secretary and continued to support the efforts of his successor Larry Summers to get it passed into law. When Clinton was asked on April 18, 2010, by ABC News' Jake Tapper if he got "bad" advice from Rubin and Summers on financial deregulations, Clinton replied, "On derivatives, yeah, I think they were wrong and I think I was wrong to take it." Astonishingly, although there was a framed copy of the pen Clinton used to sign FSMA prominently displayed in the Citigroup executive offices, neither watershed law is discussed in Rubin's memoir—an astounding omission of his historic role not noted in any major review of the book. These acts are what directly enabled the chicanery that came to dominate the activities of financial corporations, with Citigroup leading the charge to insolvency and devastation of the world economy.

After helping to get the measures into law, Rubin rode shotgun at Citigroup even as it was moving to the forefront of those mega-banking concerns rushing to take full advantage of the fantastically profitable but risky new opportunities deregulation permitted. Foremost among these was the still rapidly expanding debt securities market, born only a few years earlier. Citi was a big fish sucking up risky loans and marketing collateralized debt obligations (CDOs)—the same assets that would prove so toxic within a few short years.

In fact, Citigroup was one of the top funders of the subprime craze with $26.3 billion in subprime assets out of 350 million loan applications from 1994 to 2007, according to an analysis by the Center for Public Integrity (CPI) published May 6, 2009. While the frontline lenders were lesser-known companies, which are mostly bankrupt now, it was the big boys like Citi that backed them with the billions they needed to operate.

Out of the top twenty-five underwriters of the subprime sinkhole, Citigroup was one of only five still lending in mid-2009, thanks to government help in the form of $20 billion through the Troubled Asset Relief Program (TARP), $20 billion through the Treasury Department's "targeted investment program," and a $5-billion Treasury backstop on asset losses, as well as a guarantee of protection for a whopping $306 billion in potentially toxic assets.

The CPI report, "Who's Behind the Financial Meltdown," noted that typical of Citigroup's earlier behavior was a December 2006 prospectus in which it "pooled $492 million worth of mortgages to sell to investors as securities . . . 81 percent of the loans were adjustable rate mortgages." More than half of them were originated by now bankrupt New Century Financial Corp., a subprime loan specialist that made an astonishing $75.9 billion in loans between 2005 and 2007. Since New Century was not a bank and could not accept deposits, it needed to get its capital from the established banks, which were only too eager to write the company what seemed to be a blank check.

Citigroup's excuse for this crushing irresponsibility was straight schoolyard: Everybody was doing it.

"Demonizing the bankers as if they and they alone created the financial meltdown is both inaccurate and short-sighted," said Citigroup chair Richard Parsons on April 6, 2009. "Everybody participated in pumping up this balloon and now that the balloon has deflated, everybody in reality has some part in the blame."

Ah, except Citigroup was not a hapless member of the go-along crowd but rather a key leader in the field of predatory lending to unqualified borrowers. In 2000, it bought, for $31 billion, infamous subprime lender Associates First Capital, which just two years later earned its purchaser a

Federal Trade Commission settlement fine of $215 million for "systematic and widespread deceptive and abusive lending practices."

As the *Economist* wrote of Citi's purchase of Associates in September 2000, "it extends Citi's already huge credit card operation to a lucrative new niche (price-insensitive, if default-prone, borrowers) . . . Whether [Citi's 'upmarket image'] is compatible with high-interest lending depends on whether clients see the loans as something smart, such as 'evolved credit extension,' or something seamy such as loan-sharking. Either way, it is a money-spinner."

Consumer advocates were not pleased. "We're disappointed to see Citigroup getting into this business and to see them acquiring someone with such a poor record of treatment of consumers," Consumers Union attorney Gail Hillebrand said at the time to *Dallas Morning News* reporter Pamela Yip. "The Associates has been sued all around the country for selling consumers insurance that they don't need and which is overpriced, and for sales practices of various kinds that don't help the consumer."

To mitigate such concerns, Citi promised regulators it would improve its consumer lending practices. Watchdog groups were skeptical.

"Associates has a notable record of outrageous predatory lending practices," wrote Maude Hurd of the Association of Community Organizations for Reform Now (ACORN), in *American Banker*'s December 8, 2000, issue. "Combining this predatory lender with Citigroup looks like a recipe for further destructive behavior in low-income neighborhoods. If the deal should have been approved at all, it clearly should only have been approved on the basis of a strong and enforceable commitment to fair lending."

Even if Citigroup cleaned up Associates' behavior after buying it, the company would still have benefitted from earlier shady practices. In any case, Citi's own credibility was further eroded in May 2004, when it was fined $70 million by the Fed for abuses by CitiFinancial, another of its units that engaged in subprime lending.

As late as February 2007, with Rubin still a top honcho, Citi continued on the path to collect questionable loans by the bushel. The anatomy of one such case deserving dissection involves ACC Capital Holdings of Orange, California, the holding company for Ameriquest Mortgage and its sister firm Argent Mortgage, which together before the subprime mortgage implosion were the world's leading lender of such loans. On January 23, 2006, Ameriquest entered into a settlement with forty-nine states and the District of Columbia involving its predatory lending practices, including deception, boiler-room sales tactics, pushing consumers into mortgages they could not afford, and inflating the income of borrowers and the value of property, among other transgressions. Victims often were the poor, the elderly, and minorities.

Appointed by the five-member board of directors of ACC Capital Holdings to be liaison with the Ameriquest legal team negotiating the settlement was Deval Patrick, a close friend of Barack Obama and the Democrat elected governor of Massachusetts in 2006, who was very familiar with the company's historic problems in this area.

In 2004, around the time he was leaving his post as executive vice president and general counsel of Coca-Cola, Patrick was asked by ACC Capital founder Roland Arnall to join the board of the company, then under investigation. The men had crossed paths before. In 1996, Patrick was head of the civil rights division of the Justice Department—appointed by Clinton—which had sued Long Beach Mortgage Co., Ameriquest's corporate predecessor, for discrimination based on race, gender, age, and national origin. The firm paid $4 million to settle the case. So now Patrick was being asked to switch sides by the man his department sued, whose company was again under government investigation.

As Patrick recalled the moment for *Boston Globe* reporter Brian C. Mooney in a 2006 interview: "He [Arnall] said: 'We've started to make some changes and we're under investigation'—I think at that point it was by maybe a dozen attorneys general—'and we need to settle those and make these changes, and that's where you come in. The investigation is a platform for change.'" Patrick accepted the $360,000-a-year position.

In any case, Patrick's background paid off for ACC Capital Holdings on February 20, 2007, less than a month after Ameriquest settled its case for $325 million—and then had to find a way to pay it. It was that day that Patrick picked up the phone and called his former Clinton administration colleague Robert Rubin at Citigroup. Patrick was asked to make the call by an executive for ACC Capital, which wanted to offer Citigroup a deal in exchange for the needed cash.

Patrick had resigned from ACC's board about seven months earlier, after his association with the predatory lender became an issue in his gubernatorial campaign. His spokesman, Kyle Sullivan, told the *Boston Globe*'s Frank Phillips that in "a very short phone conversation" the governor vouched for the "current management and the character of the company . . . He did not advocate in any way for a deal between Citigroup and ACC Capital. He simply offered himself as a reference."

Nevertheless, eight days later, an ailing ACC Capital announced a deal with Citigroup, which would give the lender cash and a credit line while Citigroup would get an option to buy ACC Capital companies, excluding Ameriquest. The *New York Times* later reported that the cash totaled $100 million and was intended to allow the company to continue to make mortgage loans. Citigroup was getting into business with a company whose mortgage lenders, Argent and Ameriquest, had earned a reputation among consumer advocates as the "the worst of the worst" of subprime lenders.

By this time, Los Angeles billionaire Roland Arnall was living in the Netherlands, having been confirmed as Bush's ambassador there—Deval Patrick's letter of endorsement might have helped overcome confirmation hurdles in the Senate Foreign Relations Committee, where some Democrats were unhappy with the nominee's track record against consumers. Perhaps members of Congress were swayed by Arnall's largesse: according to the Associated Press, he was one of the top ten donors along with his wife to the Republican Party in 2003 to 2005 and gave nearly $1 million to help pay for President Bush's second-inauguration celebration.

About seven months later, on October 31, 2007, Citigroup snapped up Argent Mortgage, which was holding $45 billion in home loan debt. That same day, ACC Capital announced it was shutting down Ameriquest. According to *Inside Mortgage Finance*, the acquisition made Citigroup the second largest subprime servicer after Countrywide.

A Citi exec, Jeffrey Perlowitz, told Eric Dash of the *New York Times* that under a new name, Citi Residential, the company would continue to originate loans. "It is not going to be a subprime shop. It is going to be a nonconforming shop and we are going to originate [loans] along the continuum, from jumbo loans to Alt-A to subprime," he said in the September 1, 2007, article, which continued: "Citigroup will also take over servicing rights to ACC Capital's $45 billion mortgage portfolio, which is among the industry's biggest and most efficient. It has more than 2,000 employees in California and Illinois. The move will bolster Citigroup's payment collection abilities, giving it a special servicing ability and a bigger presence to help weather the expected surge

in delinquencies and foreclosures from a housing slump."
Maybe they anticipated slight showers, but they got slammed
by a hurricane the likes of Katrina.

As for collateralized debt obligations, a financial product
protected so aggressively by Rubin at Treasury, Citigroup
was a heavyweight underwriter. In 2006, it "just missed doubling its CDO underwriting volume year-over-year," according to an Asset Securitization Report of January 8, 2007,
bringing $36.4 billion of the sliced-and-diced loans to market
for a nearly 11 percent market share, second only to Merrill
Lynch.

In other words, Citigroup, under Saint Rubin's leadership,
was rushing to the cliff like a lemming, pouring resources
into markets that were about to collapse. And, it would be
reported, Rubin was whipping the firm on its suicide race.

But even Rubin, celebrated in the media as being almost
terminally unflappable, must have had a stirring of "what
hath I wrought?" discomfort in September 2007, as the mortgage meltdown was gaining serious momentum. After all,
he presents himself as far more than just another Wall Street
gambler, repeatedly emphasizing in his writings his role in
public policy and waxing ever so modestly about his vast experience in predicting the future of markets.

At a dramatic meeting that month, described by an atyp-
ically critical *New York Times* report, Citigroup's top execs
were briefed on the true scope of the corporation's massive
exposure to the high-risk loan portfolios belatedly deemed

to be toxic. Called into an emergency gathering in the wood-paneled library, CEO Charles O. Prince III supposedly "learned for the first time," according to the *Times*' insider sources, that the bank owned about $43 billion in dubious mortgage-related assets. Huge losses from these mortgage securities would soon trigger a dizzying fall for "the nation's largest and mightiest financial institution," with Citigroup's stock value plunging more than 90 percent in just two years, from $244 billion to a mere $20.5 billion in November 2008.

The *Times* article, published November 23, 2008, and titled "Citigroup Saw No Red Flags Even as It Made Bolder Bets," finds "Citigroup insiders" blaming a lack of checks and balances within the bank. The story found that those charged with overseeing deals (and regulating pay structures) were so hungry to make short-term profits, they neglected to manage their colleagues who were making bad deals.

Such a problem might have reminded Rubin of his role in ending Depression-era legislation that had imposed such checks and balances, especially the division between the collection of bank deposits and the sellers of securities. We can't know, because Rubin refused to comment for the report, a mere five months after a lavish *Times* profile. Back then, on April 27, 2008, in a story headlined "Where Was the Wise Man?" the paper of record's business section was still treating Rubin with kid gloves, allowing him to glibly disavow responsibility for Citigroup's growing troubles, without challenge. Had Rubin made any mistakes?

Rubin responded, "I've thought about that. I honestly don't know. In hindsight, there are a lot of things we'd do differently. But in the context of the facts as I knew them and my role, I'm inclined to think probably not."

That Rubin was so blatantly skating past the growing wreckage around him was rather nonchalantly, if oxymoronically, accepted by *Times* business reporters Nelson D. Schwartz and Eric Dash. "Modest and genial to a fault, Mr. Rubin is also proud and protective of his sterling reputation," they wrote, noting that "adorning a wall behind his desk is a framed *Time* cover from 1999 hailing his role on what the magazine called the 'Committee to Save the World.'" The *Times* reference to Rubin's "sterling reputation" does not seem intended as sarcasm.

But a few months later, accelerating events—and a massive taxpayer bailout of the company—no doubt led the *Times* to produce what amounted to a much more critical investigation into Rubin's apparently less-than-sterling role in the bank's collapse.

"The bank's downfall was years in the making and involved many in its hierarchy, particularly Mr. Prince and Robert E. Rubin, an influential director and senior adviser," wrote reporters Eric Dash and Julie Creswell in the November 22 story. Sources at Citigroup said Rubin and Prince were at fault for many of the problems facing the bank at the time—as the two of them had choreographed and endorsed the strategy of over-leveraging for the sake of higher profits.

That mighty Citigroup had to be teetering on the edge of bankruptcy and be bailed out by the U.S. government for the country's most respected news organization to get serious about reporting on such an influential man is astonishing. The *Times* waited until late 2008 to finally carry a major piece connecting Rubin's performance in government with his subsequent employment at Citigroup; suddenly the newspaper was acknowledging a connection between Rubin's role in government and the disaster that had befallen the bank he helped lead after returning to the private sector. During Rubin's time at the Treasury under Bill Clinton, the *Times* said, he helped repeal banking regulation dating back to the Great Depression. This effort paved the way for the creation of Citigroup, as Rubin's "reforms" encouraged banks to become more than lenders—to be traffickers in new kinds of financial products. During the Clinton years Rubin fought to curb oversight of these "exotic" products.

"And since joining Citigroup in 1999 as a trusted adviser to the bank's senior executives," the *Times* report explained, "Mr. Rubin, who is an economic adviser on the transition team of President-elect Barack Obama, has sat atop a bank that has been roiled by one financial miscue after another."

Not only was Rubin on the transition team, but it was his protégés Timothy Geithner and Lawrence Summers who secured the two top economic jobs in the new Obama administration. Rubin had pushed Geithner to be chair of the New York Fed, in which capacity he conveniently helped concoct the bailout that saved Citigroup from bankruptcy. Summers, as the Treasury secretary who succeeded Rubin, had been, if anything, even more aggressive than Rubin in pushing for the deregulatory policies that enabled Citigroup to stumble so badly.

And stumble it did. Rubin's role extended beyond just the laws he had helped pass. Charles Prince, the boss at Citi's corporate and investment bank since 2003, looked to the more experienced Rubin for leadership. The *Times* quoted an unnamed Citi executive: "Chuck was totally new to the job. He didn't know a CDO from a grocery list, so he looked for someone for advice and support. That person was Rubin. And Rubin had always been an advocate of being more aggressive in the capital markets arena. He would say, 'You have to take more risk if you want to earn more.'"

From 2003 to 2005, Citigroup more than tripled its issuance of CDOs to $20 billion, generating up to $500 million in fees from the business in 2005 alone. The biggest financial services company in the world was following the blueprint set in motion two decades earlier by the architect of its rise, Sandy Weill: growth at all costs. It was decided to doubledown on the CDO market, rather than hold tight. As the *Times'* Eric Dash and Julie Creswell reported, in 2005 Rubin helped draft the blueprints for large internal expansions at Citigroup. According to current and former colleagues, he worried that Citigroup was lagging behind competitors like Goldman Sachs, so he advocated for the company to take on more high-growth fixed-income trading, including more collateralized debt obligations. Dash and Creswell's sources said Rubin wanted Citigroup to take on more and more risk—with the vague notion that this was contingent on increased oversight as well; after the fact, the Federal Reserve concluded that oversight had been woefully inadequate. At the time, however, Citigroup consolidated its strategy, and Rubin worked with Prince to bolster the confidence of the board.

As its CDO business was ramping up, Citi "used accounting maneuvers to move billions of dollars of the troubled assets off its books, freeing capital so the bank could grow even larger," according to the *Times.* Yet again we see the limitations of the corporate self-regulation touted by free-market purists like Greenspan: Nobody, whatever their job title at Citi, wanted to dam this river of cash that was doubling and tripling bonuses for traders.

"I just think senior managers got addicted to the revenues and arrogant about the risks they were running," a *Times* source inside Citi's CDO group told the paper. "As long as you could grow revenues, you could keep your bonus growing."

In fact, almost up to the moment Citigroup acknowledged in November 2007 it would write down some $8 billion to $11 billion in worthless assets, its executives clung to the belief that CDOs were not risky. A key fault in this faith was that much of Citi's CDO sales were in a form called a "CDO liquidity put," which would allow investors to sell them back to the bank at cost. With the economy swirling down the toilet, investors rushed to do just that, slamming Citi with $25 billion in losses, according to *Newsweek*.

Over the next eighteen months things would get much, much worse—and taxpayers would be forced to bail out Rubin's bank. Rubin told *Newsweek* and others the recession could be blamed on an economic "perfect storm." He also denied he led Citi over the edge, claiming he was too ignorant of newfangled markets to have pushed the company in a particular direction.

"Actually, I'm probably close to twenty years beyond which I had a granular knowledge [of financial details]," he told *Newsweek*'s Evan Thomas and Michael Hirsh in an article published December 8, 2008. With an all-too-convenient modesty the reporters blithely accepted: "Rubin may not fully grasp what he has helped bring about—that the unregulated markets he and Greenspan embraced so completely a decade ago are out of control."

Rarely has there been a clearer case of a conflict of interest between public service and private-sector reward than Rubin's support of radical bank deregulation as Treasury secretary in between stints at two of the most powerful banks in history. Yet the only time a potential conflict of interest concerning Rubin's whirling through the revolving door between government and business surfaced in the mass media was in relation to an important but limited example of such conflict—his role in Citigroup's attempt to save a crashing Enron.

As detailed in the previous chapter, radical state and federal deregulation had been key to Enron's booming growth from a power producer and deliverer to a trading company profiting by making bets on the rise and fall of the very energy prices they were manipulating. In particular, a provision stuck into the CFMA directly at Enron's behest by Phil Gramm gave the company free rein.

Rubin was already at Citigroup when the CFMA passed, but he strongly supported the entire bill, and it was his protégé and replacement as Treasury secretary, Lawrence Summers, along with Gramm and Fed chair Alan Greenspan, who midwifed its birth. Had this off-stage role been Rubin's only public connection with Enron, his role in Citigroup's substantial involvement with the company probably would have gone unnoticed. As with much news reporting, however, the larger truths are often ignored until crystallized in a single incident. The "hook" for questions about the extent of Rubin's far-reaching pull inside both government and the financial sector was the phone call detailed in the previous chapter that he made to the undersecretary of the Treasury, Peter Fisher, on behalf of Enron, the company already nationally famous for its bad behavior.

When Enron—which only two years earlier was a Wall Street darling with unparalleled Beltway influence—fell into a rapid death spiral at the end of 2001, Citigroup rushed to its aid. Rubin's role was both to be expected and unethical; one of the key assets he brought to the executive suite was his enormous knowledge of, and influence with, key government agencies and regulators, many of whom recently had worked for him. Even during the new administration of George W. Bush, Rubin was not without significant clout.

So it was that Rubin, on November 8, 2001, acted on behalf of Enron by making that call to his former associate Peter Fisher at the Treasury Department, asking him to intervene with the credit agencies in an action critical to the survival of the company. Later, embarrassed, Rubin would claim to have been acting on behalf of the public and greater good, as if above the normal restrictions and morality related to conflict of interest.

As we know, the immediate issue that pushed Rubin to use his power of access was the prospect of credit rating agencies, led by Moody's, downgrading Enron's stock to junk status. He later would explain in his memoir that he was trying to give banks more time to prepare a "rescue package" to keep the company functioning. In addition, he wrote that he was trying to protect a possible merger deal between Enron and energy rival Dynegy—without noting that Citigroup stood to make tens of millions of dollars as a fee for facilitating it. Downgrading of Enron's credit rating would "doom a Dynegy merger and lead to Enron's collapse," Rubin wrote. Not to mention hurting Citigroup.

"In that context, I placed a call to Peter Fisher, a senior official at the Treasury Department, whom I had known when he was at the Federal Reserve Bank of New York. I asked

Peter whether he thought it would make sense for him or someone else at Treasury to place a call to the rating agencies and suggest briefly holding off on any downgrade of Enron's debt while the banks considered putting in more money."

In a gross understatement, Rubin conceded that Citigroup was "a creditor of Enron and would ultimately recognize losses on that position." Indeed, Citigroup's loan to the energy company was $1 billion, a sum that was at huge risk if the credit rating were downgraded and the company tanked.

According to a staff report of the Senate Governmental Affairs Committee, Rubin was asked to make the call to Fisher by Michael A. Carpenter, then head of Citigroup's investment banking unit. Yet in his memoir, Rubin made a point to stress his selfless in-the-public-interest motive for the call—that Enron's collapse could have had implications beyond the energy firm: "Many feared that the economy as a whole could take a significant hit as well." He noted "the important public policy concern about the energy markets—not just a parochial concern about Citigroup's exposure."

As we know, Fisher rejected the idea and reported the call to his superiors. But Rubin, while conceding then that it was "probably a bad idea," in his memoir defended the ethics involved.

"Disingenuous" is the defining word for Rubin here. What nonsense to suggest that "an important public policy concern" led to the call when it was in fact the "parochial concern about Citigroup's exposure" that was at work here. How

parochial is in the mind of the beholder, but surely even for
bankers of Rubin's grandeur the potential loss of $1 billion
would seem major. And his rationale that he was concerned
about the flow of energy supplies seems downright deceitful
when we remember that Enron had been profiting enormously from disrupting energy supplies in order to game
prices and put the squeeze on California.

"If Rubin had succeeded in persuading Fisher to intervene
with Moody's, an independent credit-rating company, Citigroup would have been able to minimize its losses by dump-
ing its bad Enron credit on unwitting investors," argued
author Mark R. Levin, writing in the conservative *National
Review Online*, in a January 3, 2003, commentary. "Talk about
insider trading!"

While Levin clearly has a partisan axe to grind, even for
Rubin's defenders in the "neutral" media, especially at the
New York Times, this was a rare blemish on the Wall Street
Galahad.

On February 11, 2002, the *Times* covered the controversial
Rubin-Fisher phone call. But conservative *Forbes* magazine
media critic Mark Lewis chided *Times* reporters Joseph Kahn
and Alessandra Stanley for letting Rubin off easy by asserting
that the call "will probably be no more than a footnote in
the Enron story." He also criticized them for seeming to minimize the obvious conflict while fretting that Rubin "inad-
vertently gave comfort to the [Bush] White House and to
some conservative commentators," who made hay out of

the prominent Democrat's support for Enron. "Today, the *Times* finally turned the spotlight on Rubin," Lewis wrote, "but the story amounted to a glowing profile of the former Clinton Administration official, wrapped around a gentle admonishment for his Enron involvement. And the *Times* seemed less concerned that Rubin had done anything wrong than that he had given aid and comfort to Republicans by making this a bipartisan scandal."

In his book, Rubin takes pride in the fact that a Senate committee, headed by Joe Lieberman, that investigated the affair agreed that he acted within the law. However, he was basically cleared on a technicality: The law only bars former officials from dealing with their previous government agency for a certain amount of time; the Rubin call was made after that deadline. Ironically, as the *Economist* reported on January 17, 2002, "what he did was legal, but only because Bill Clinton, in his last days as president, cancelled an executive order that barred top officials from lobbying their old department for five years after leaving office. The order was in place throughout Mr. Rubin's tenure at Treasury."

It is important to make the Enron-Citigroup connection, not just because Rubin is still such an influential figure who needs to be held accountable, but also because it is a key to understanding the economic collapse. Both humongous companies were allowed to grow beyond the point where they could be effectively regulated by government (or, arguably, by their own management team). Their collapse impoverished tens of thousands of shareholders and employees who were deceived by executives posing as competent and honest professionals. What were they thinking, these corporate titans, as they led or oversaw the massive risks that brought them to ruin in astonishing fashion?

While there are lawsuits still pending concerning Citigroup's involvement with Enron, the legal reckoning is limited. It is "really hard to sue lawyers and investment bankers under the securities fraud statues," Franklin B. Velie, a former prosecutor and one of the top experts in this area, told the *Washington Times*. "You have to prove that a defendant was actually part of the fraud" and not merely negligent.

That is the obstacle faced by lawyers, led by the University of California's pension fund but representing thousands of Enron shareholders, who are trying to hold Citigroup accountable for damages as part of a larger suit against Enron. The complex case is winding its way through the courts, but whatever the outcome, the 485-page complaint filed in U.S. District Court makes a compelling case for linking the deregulation of banks to the larger economic crisis. According to the complaint, "The banks named as defendants evolved into their present structure in anticipation of and after the repeal of the Glass-Steagall Act in '99, which allowed financial enterprises again to offer both commercial and investment services—a practice which had been outlawed for 60 years." The complaint quoted a *Business Week* article from March 25, 2002, which reported that bankers "said" that they would "erect so-called Chinese walls that forbade sharing information between those selling a company's stock and those arguing its financing."

But, it was noted, those barriers are permeable.

> Chinese walls are porous. Bankers ignore them when
> it's convenient: They take analysts on roadshows of in-
> vestment-banking clients—their way of making it clear
> they don't want downgrades of those companies. The
> walls also provide cover for bankers, who let analysts
> push a client's stock even when they know the com-
> pany is in trouble. That's why analysts recommended
> Enron to the end, though the bankers behind its com-
> plex financing knew it was on the skids.

Citigroup was vital to the funding of that complex financing. Quoting the Dow Jones News Service of February 26, 2002, the complaint notes: "Between them, Citigroup and JP Morgan/Chase served as lead manager on more than $20 billion in syndicated bank loans to Enron over the past decade, with Citigroup also underwriting more than $4 billion in stock and bond offerings for the company."

With Rubin's Citigroup having such a huge investment in the flailing firm, one would have to be exceedingly gullible to believe his pleas to Treasury to intervene on behalf of Enron were the act of a wise do-gooder. However, beyond previous credit arrangements, which would have given it the clout to inspect Enron's books much earlier, Citigroup was also actively and deeply involved in Enron's endgame, making a further mockery of Rubin's claim to be above the fray. The legal brief lays out clearly what Rubin pointedly ignores in his book:

> In late 11/01, JPMorgan and Citigroup were desperately trying to arrange the sale of Enron to Dynegy so they could split a $90 million fee and so Enron would not go bankrupt, which they knew would lead to suits over, and investigations into, their prior deals with Enron—which they knew would be highly embarrassing and could expose them to massive liability to third parties and subordination of their creditor claims against Enron. Their scheme could not succeed without keeping Enron's investment-grade credit rating in place until the sale to Dynegy could be completed. So, on or about 11/8/01, Rubin, the vice chairman of Citigroup, and Harrison, the chairman of JPMorgan, called Moody's—a key rating agency—and pressured Moody's to keep Enron's investment grade credit rating in place until JPMorgan and Citigroup could complete the sale of Enron to Dynegy.

Thus, not only was Rubin calling his old offices at Treasury, but he called Moody's directly. Apparently he had a lot of time to donate to the public good that month.

Regardless—and Moody's did soften its downgrade of Enron enough to keep it from falling below "investment grade"—the deal fell apart when Dynegy discovered just how horrid was Enron's balance sheet, which had been concealed by fraudulent accounting sanctioned by accounting giant Arthur Andersen. That Dynegy could figure this out in a matter of days but Rubin and Citigroup couldn't over several years almost defies logical explanation.

"Citigroup's relationships with Enron were so extensive that senior executives at Citigroup constantly interacted with top executives of Enron, i.e., Lay, Skilling, Richard A. Causey, Jeffrey McMahon or Andrew Fastow, on almost a daily basis," the University of California brief claims, arguing that Citigroup was in so deep with Enron that it had to know the company's dark truths. According to the brief:

> Citigroup actively engaged and participated in the fraudulent scheme and furthered Enron's fraudulent course of conduct and business in several ways. It participated in loans of over $4 billion to Enron, . . . helped Enron raise over $2 billion from the investing public via the sale of securities, . . . helped it structure and finance certain of the illicit SPEs [special purpose entities] and partnerships Enron controlled which were a primary vehicle utilized by Enron to falsify its reported financial results, and engaged in transactions

with Enron to disguise loans to Enron and thus enable
Enron to falsify its true financial condition, liquidity
and creditworthiness.

The brief notes that Citigroup's extensive involvement
with Enron was not the work of a few bad apples or a single
division that flew under the radar: "In interacting with
Enron, Citigroup functioned as a consolidated and unified
entity. There was no so-called 'Chinese Wall' to seal off the
Citigroup securities analysis from the information which Citigroup obtained in rendering commercial and investment
banking services to Enron."

Other questionable practices exposed after Enron crashed
included the fact, according to the *New York Times* on July
23, 2002, that "senior credit officers of Citigroup misrepresented the full nature of a 1999 transaction with Enron in
the records of the deal so that the energy company could ignore accounting requirements and hide its true financial condition, according to internal bank documents and
government investigators." This allowed Enron to keep $125
million in debt off its books. Consider, too, that even as it
helped hide the reality behind Enron's façade, Citigroup was
actually covering its own bottom line by hedging—betting
against it with $1.4 billion in securities that offset its exposure
to Enron's bankruptcy.

"Citigroup refused this week to answer repeated questions about its choice of timing, except to say that it had intended to hedge its existing and potential future exposure to

Enron," reported the *Times* on February 8, 2002. "It acknowl-edged that the hedge was its largest against any company."

In other words, with the sainted Rubin aboard in a top role, Citigroup had used its political and economic capital to fuel Enron's rise, helped it hide its spiraling debt, and tried to manipulate the government and rating agencies to con-ceal its imminent doom from the common investor and company employee. Over eight years, Rubin was paid one-eighth of $1 billion from Citigroup, even as it was heading for the shoals of destruction enabled by the deregulation he pushed while in the Clinton administration.

Bizarrely, despite all the press coverage Enron's corruption earned, Citigroup's deep involvement, well known since 2002, in no significant way appears to have affected Rubin's esteem or credibility in the media or within the Democratic Party. Nor did the developing mortgage derivatives crash that would gut Citigroup keep Rubin and his protégés from again serving as the go-to economic experts for Democratic candidates, espe-cially the original front-runner, Hillary Clinton, and, later, the eventual winner of the White House, Barack Obama.

"Everyone agrees we have to save Citi, so we're throwing hundreds of billions at it because it was so poorly managed, and yet there's Robert Rubin sitting right there in the middle of it and he's been looked to as a wise man," Dean Baker, cofounder of the left-leaning Center for Economic and Pol-icy Research, told *Newsweek*. "It's outrageous. We're turning to the same people who made this mess in the first place."

CHAPTER 7

Poverty Pimps

It's the same the whole world over
It's the poor what gets the blame
It's the rich what gets the pleasure
Ain't it all a bloomin' shame?

That chorus of the nineteenth-century Cockney ditty "She Was Poor But She Was Honest," detailing the travails of a poor lass whose life is ruined by the deflowering advances of a rich man, best captures the mainstream Republican response to the banking meltdown. Their defense has been to blame "bleeding-heart" liberals concerned for the poor for a debacle that occurred unmistakably on the GOP's watch, and in response to their antiregulatory ideology, but for which they shuddered to take responsibility.

The effort to shift blame from Wall Street moguls to the poor who took loans they could not afford, while illogical given the frenzy with which those loans were marketed, is also understandable as an act of political desperation. Blame those being swindled rather than the swindlers has been the mantra of America's right wing, bereft of any other explanation for the debacle that will allow them to continue their ways.

The Wall Street meltdown left conservative politicians and their ancillary pundits in the lurch looking for a culprit, any culprit—except the folks who run Wall Street, that powerful emblem and engine of American capitalism. Instead, they settled on an alternate bogeyman: government efforts to end discrimination in the mortgage markets and broaden home ownership to low- and moderate-income families.

The problem with the economy, they argued, was not greed or incompetence in the executive suites, but a misguided pressure to lend money to irresponsible poor and nonwhite people. Government influence on the mortgage markets, the logic went, had distorted the markets and created an unstable base of bad loans that, like a foundation made of sand, had sent the global economy sliding off a cliff at the first hard rain.

When the Bush administration was forced in the fall of 2008 to bail out the "government sponsored enterprises" or GSEs, as the mortgage buying companies of Fannie Mae and Freddie Mac are referred to, grateful conservatives finally had what appeared to be a convenient government villain. Working backward from the GSEs' founding mandate to support the market for middle- and low-income buyers by buying up mortgages from lenders and then repackaging them as securities, longtime critics were only too excited to blame do-gooder liberalism as the fly in the ointment of capitalism. Specifically, House Financial Services Committee chair Barney Frank was singled out as having pressured the GSEs to make loans to unqualified poor people—especially minorities—who then defaulted and caused the economic downturn.

"Taxpayers are now on the hook for as much as $200 billion to rescue Fannie Mae and Freddie Mac, and if you want to know why, look no further than the rapid response to this bailout from House baron Barney Frank," wrote the *Wall Street Journal* in a September 9, 2008, editorial. "Mr. Frank wants you to pick up the tab for its failures, while he still vows to block a reform that might prevent the same disaster from happening again."

The editorial is worth quoting at length because it summarizes a perspective broadly held and argued by conservatives. It correctly criticizes Frank for statements he made in 2004, when Fannie Mae revealed a "multibillion-dollar financial 'misstatement.'" Frank had said that he felt that despite this, the mortgage lender was not a danger to taxpayers. "I think Wall Street will get over it," Frank had said. The *Journal* mocked this response—"Yes they're certainly 'over it' . . .

now that Uncle Sam is guaranteeing their Fannie paper, and even Fannie's subordinated debt." The newspaper then ridiculed Frank for his criticism of conservative economic policies, saying that what really blocked reform was Frank's insistence that "any reform be watered down and not include any reduction in their MBS [mortgage backed security] holdings."

Some liberal pundits, most notably the *New York Times*' Paul Krugman, attempted to play down the role of Freddie and Fannie, arguing, incorrectly, that they only made proper "conforming" loans. But that was false, for the definition of conforming is whatever Freddie and Fannie approved of, and those turned out to be as disastrously irresponsible as any.

The free-market conservatives are right in criticizing those GSEs, for they were highly culpable, and the grand swindle could not have taken place without them. But they are wrong in describing the GSEs led by Fannie Mae and Freddie Mac as do-gooder public entities; in reality they are privately owned, profit-driven companies that richly reward their executives for stock market success. That is the source of much confusion in this debate; the top executives of the GSEs were compensated as handsomely, and often more so, than any other corporate executives, but because of their original government sponsorship, they made for convenient targets for the wrath of free-market ideologues.

The man who understood that best was a whistleblower in the mold of Brooksley Born. Like her, Armando Falcon

Jr. was appointed by the president to regulate entities led by people who had the political clout to prevent any meaningful regulation. Falcon was director of the Office of Federal Housing Enterprise Oversight (OFHEO), the underfunded and weak government agency assigned to monitor the federal housing behemoths.

Thus there was considerable irony when, a year and a half after the crash he had warned against, Falcon found himself on April 9, 2010, before the bipartisan Financial Crisis Inquiry Commission, which included Brooksley Born, unraveling his part of this tale of woe. His testimony was a devastating indictment of the culture of corruption that was as bipartisan in origin as was the makeup of the commission now seeking answers. He had attempted to regulate agencies dominated by leaders drawn from Democratic ranks during a Republican administration, but as with Born earlier, he was done in by both sides.

Yet while Falcon had come to be supported by conservatives who never did have much love for the hybrid GSEs he was attempting to regulate, he was clear that the cause was not the pathetic ambitions of the ordinary folks attempting to buy homes they couldn't properly afford. Rather, it was the greed of the powerful. Falcon cut through the false dichotomy that cast blame for the banking debacle either on the huge totally private financial moguls or their government-sponsored rivals but not both. He said they were, in terms of motivation and impact, one and the same.

As stated, conservatives make much of the affordable housing goals of the GSEs, endorsed by George W. Bush as well as Bill Clinton, as the cause of the irresponsible lending that occurred these past decades. But Falcon in his testimony shot that one down. Asked by the commission to testify on the impact of those goals on the GSE issue, Falcon responded: "Your letter also asked me about the impact of affordable housing goals on the enterprises' financial problems. In my opinion, the goals were not the cause of the enterprises' demise. The firms would not engage in any activity, goal fulfilling or otherwise, unless there was a profit to be made. Fannie and Freddie invested in subprime and Alt A mortgages in order to increase profits and regain market share. Any impact on meeting affordable housing goals was a byproduct of the activity."

Nevertheless, it remains true that the GSEs were the major purchasers and packagers of securities based on mortgages, and they acted with the implicit guarantee that the bonds they sold were backed by the federal government. When the meltdown occurred, that guarantee went from implicit to explicit, and the federal government moved in and backed all of those toxic obligations. It also fueled the conservative attack that two key executives of Fannie Mae, the larger of the two agencies, were also influential players within the earlier Clinton administration and had led the fight to prevent any meaningful regulation of those mortgage-based securities. What the conservatives insist on ignoring is that while Fannie and Freddie were originally government sponsored to make moderate-priced housing more accessible, they had long since shed any of the trappings or restraints of a government agency.

Over the decades since 1938, when Fannie Mae, the first of the GSEs, was created, they had in effect gone from being public to private enterprises, with the companies' and their top executives' fortunes dependent on stock market valuation of their publicly traded shares.

In that spirit, the top officials of the two agencies were rewarded not in the manner of heads of huge government agencies but rather received many times the highest pay of any such executive, including the president himself. But they did still require the acquiescence of Congress, which retained the power to pull their federal charters through legislation. Preventing that outcome, or indeed any serious regulation of the GSEs, became the major object of their lavishly funded lobbying operation. Not surprisingly then, the top executives tended to be drawn from the ranks of political operatives rather than from more traditional financial backgrounds. It is also true, as conservatives are wont to point out, that the two men who most shaped the actions of Fannie Mae, the more powerful of the two agencies, were drawn from the Democratic side. But they couldn't have done this damage to the housing market alone and instead functioned like, and indeed were in close partnership with, the other moguls in the mortgage business.

The tale of their alliance with leaders of a runaway mortgage industry, particularly the industry-dominant figure of
Countrywide's Angelo Mozilo, who also cofounded subprime sinkhole IndyMac Bank, which failed as well, is central
to the debacle that ensued. But to mention the guys on the
quasi-government-sponsored side and not their key partners
in the fully privatized mortgage business is to deny reality.

In fact, it is the dance of the private with the public that
is the norm in what we naïvely refer to as our "free enterprise system"—be it agribusiness, the defense industry,
telecommunications, or, as in this case, the financial sector.
All of these industries operate in an environment of government rules that their lobbyists get to help write, and all succeed through an ability to negotiate the regulatory
environment that results from those laws.

At this dance, Countrywide's Mozilo was a virtuoso, but
he had two key partners every bit as skilled as he was on the
GSE side of things. During the past two decades, one of the
two main leaders of the government-sponsored agencies was
James A. Johnson, who started political life working for Min-
nesota Democratic senator and later vice president Walter
Mondale and parlayed that into a job running Fannie Mae
that paid him more than $6 million a year.

The *Washington Post* in a fawning tribute to Johnson on
March 27, 1998, shortly before he retired from Fannie Mae,
referred to him as "one of the most powerful men in the
United States." The *Post*'s reporter added: "As chairman of

three preeminent institutions in the nation's capital—the government-sponsored home mortgage behemoth known as Fannie Mae, the peerless think tank known as the Brookings Institution, and the mammoth performing arts emporium known as the Kennedy Center—he has positioned himself to exert enormous influence over the country's economic, intellectual and cultural lives. And while he's at it, he's getting seriously rich."

A far less flattering portrait a year earlier by Matthew Cooper in *Slate*, titled "A Medici with Your Money," pointed out, "he is not a philanthropist with his own money. The fount of Johnson's generosity is Fannie Mae's foundation, funded out of its profits." The *Slate* article had it right, noting the connection between the vast public outreach of Johnson's operation and his goal of retaining government backing for an enormous engine of profit from which he benefitted mightily: "What makes Fannie Mae special is that it is essentially the taxpayers' money that Johnson is giving away. Fannie Mae enjoys a massive government subsidy, and its charitable contributions are part of a vital corporate strategy to keep it that way."

Johnson's expansive public relations strategy was maintained, indeed expanded, by the man who would replace him, his deputy Franklin Delano Raines. Prior to working for Johnson, Raines had been highly compensated as a Wall Street financial executive. At Fannie Mae he was earning $2.25 million when Clinton appointed him to be director of the Office of Management and Budget at an annual salary of $148,400. The president quipped that Raines would be joining "other successful people who came into this Administration to help save the middle class and when they leave they will be part of it."

Not quite. After Raines left two years later in 1998 and replaced Johnson as the chair of Fannie Mae, he would be paid $36 million in compensation for his last three years of service, which extended well into the Bush years, before being forced out in 2004 amid an accounting scandal. He left with a $25-million pension, an $8.7-million deferred compensation plan, another $5.5 million in stock options, and a guaranteed annual income of $1.4 million, which would be paid to him and his wife until both died. Is that what Bill Clinton considers middle class?

A year before the scandal broke and four years before Fannie Mae was revealed as a disaster case—and taken over by the federal government even as its stock shares tumbled 90 percent—Raines was much celebrated as a typical elitist progressive "doing well by doing good." Raised in a working-class family with a janitor father who built a home with his bare hands and struggled to keep a roof over his family's head, Raines's story made for great profile copy on NPR and in such national publications as the *New York Times* and *Ebony* magazine. More important, it gave Fannie Mae credibility in saying its huge expansion in alternative lending—boldly labeled the "American Dream Initiative"—was for progressive ends: helping the poor and minorities become homeowners.

Yet when the banking meltdown predictably occurred, based on years of high-risk lending and Wall Street gambling, those were the two groups hardest hit, with most who had signed up for the program losing everything. At no point in the glowing profiles of the "first African American Fortune 500 CEO" did any of those journalists use the words "predatory lending" or, at a minimum, query Raines as to the efficacy, let alone morality, of his huge compensation being tied to backing high-risk loans that should never have been made.

A significant percentage of those loans were made by Countrywide, whose chair and founder, Angelo Mozilo, had a particularly cozy relationship to Fannie Mae under both Johnson and Raines. Indeed, too cozy we would come to find out, when it was later revealed that both men had received low-interest mortgage loans from Countrywide on various houses they owned around the country. They received this favorable treatment as part of the "Friends of Angelo" program, as it was referred to internally at Countrywide. Because of all this, there is no doubt that both Raines and Johnson deserve the opprobrium heaped on them by conservatives. They are indeed "poverty pimps," who, in the imagery of the 1960s, are like the hustlers in poorer communities who rip off well-intentioned poverty programs and thus do a deep disservice to those they gave lip service to caring about.

Where the conservatives went wrong, however, is in describing this exploitation as the result of pressure from what

they claim are bleeding-heart liberals in the Clinton administration and afterward, with Frank acting as ringleader from
his powerful perch in the House finance committee. The assumption they make is that Fannie and Freddie got into trouble because of pressure to support loans to people who
shouldn't have been given loans, and therefore had stopped
acting as responsible loan guarantors of last resort. That is
exactly wrong; the problem is quite the opposite. The GSEs
simply acted all too much like any other financial conglomerate lining the pockets of their top executives—trading
short-term gain for long-term instability.

The key to Fannie Mae's explosive growth in the backing
of suspect mortgages in the 1990s rested in the decision of
its chair, Johnson, to team up with Countrywide's Angelo
Mozilo, which would lead to Fannie Mae's endorsement of
a computerized scheme to make suspect mortgages seem
credible by changing the ways that creditworthiness was
evaluated. The scheme, and that was what it unmistakably
was, revolved around something called the "CLUES system,"
a computer program Countrywide had developed that
crunched data on the creditworthiness of potential homebuyers to bypass the evaluation of loan officers as to the
creditworthiness of mortgage customers.

As Gretchen Morgenson would describe it in an August
26, 2007, *New York Times* article, as Countrywide was slith-
ering into oblivion: "Countrywide's entire operation, from
its computer system to its incentive pay structure and financ-

ing arrangements, is intended to wring maximum profits out of the mortgage lending boom no matter what it costs borrowers, according to interviews with former employees and brokers who worked in different units of the company and internal documents they provided."

Just how unsavory an operation Countrywide, the nation's top mortgage lender, had run was laid out in that article as well as congressional and SEC investigations, as Countrywide came to be absorbed by Bank of America in a shotgun marriage arranged by the U.S. government in an attempt to save both. Johnson, who was chosen by Barack Obama to head the committee vetting his vice presidential choices, had to resign that post after the *Wall Street Journal* revealed his "sweetheart" loans of more than $5 million from Countrywide as a "Friend of Angelo." Scant attention was paid, however, to the role of Mozilo in leading Fannie Mae into its downfall.

The connection between Mozilo and Johnson was as tight as it gets in their world. In 1996, as the subprime scandal was forming, Johnson named Mozilo to be chair of Fannie Mae's National Advisory Council. The purpose of that body, as announced in the Fannie Mae press release, was "to advise the corporation on issues affecting the housing and mortgage finance industry and the expansion of home ownership opportunities." And opportunities there were, as Mozilo pointed the way for Fannie Mae, providing it with an edge over its smaller and more cautious rival, Freddy Mac. A retrospective analysis by knowledgeable *National Mortgage News* executive editor Paul Muolo in May 2009 put the history of that connection clearly:

> It was no secret in the industry that Freddie Mac officials (pre being taken over by the government) were unhappy that Countrywide sold most of its residential loans to Fannie Mae. And that was by design, really. In the early 1990s, under the direction of then Fannie CEO/chairman Jim Johnson, Countrywide's founder and CEO Angelo Mozilo was actively courted and wined and dined (so to speak) by the GSE. The reason was simple: Mozilo's Countrywide was the largest residential lender in the nation. The more loans it funded—the more loans it could (in theory) sell to Fannie (as opposed to Freddie) . . . For years the running joke in the industry was that Countrywide was really a subsidiary of Fannie Mae.

On July 9, 1999, Countrywide issued a press release that laid out just how cozy the relationship had become. Entitled "Countrywide Announces Strategic Agreement with Fannie Mae," the press release began with the following: "Countrywide . . . the nation's largest independent residential mortgage lender and servicer, announced today that it has entered into a new strategic agreement with Fannie Mae that unites their unique and complementary strengths to expand markets, reduce the costs of homeownership, and to lead the mortgage industry to higher levels of productivity, efficiency and innovation."

And profit, which of course was at the heart of this "strategic agreement" between the very-much-for-profit private lender and the very-much-for-profit but government-sponsored Fannie Mae. The difference is that when the scam exploded, the federal government stepped in directly, using hundred of billions of taxpayer dollars to take over Fannie Mae, but also indirectly by providing funding for Bank of America's takeover of Countrywide.

The key to the strategic agreement was in Fannie Mae's endorsing Countrywide's computer rating scheme that bypassed traditional credit checks by experienced loan officers that for the previous lengthy history of the nation's housing industry had kept the mortgage industry solvent. As the Countrywide press release crowed: "The strategic agreement also addresses loan products and processes. The objective is to expand markets to accommodate more customers and streamline loan processing in order to reduce the up-front cost of homeownership. This entails increased acceptance of Countrywide's proprietary CLUES underwriting technology, greater use of short form appraisals, expansion of streamlined home products, flow sales for expanded criteria loans, and guideline waivers."

With those words, the mortgage lender and the government-sponsored agency sealed their deal with the devil; the wraps of reasonable restraint, due diligence of asset appraisal, verifiable credit checking, and all of the other bylaws of prudent banking were lifted, and the gold rush was on. Nor did the principals care much about the obvious risk in which they were engaging, since they assumed it would be passed on long before the consequences of such irresponsible behavior were felt. That was because of the wonders of securitization of debt to be sold in that unregulated commodities market, which seventeen months later the Commodity Futures Modernization Act signed by Clinton would guarantee to remain unregulated.

The press release marked this enormous shift in the marketing of mortgages, quoting Mozilo: "This new strategic agreement between Fannie Mae and Countrywide is an unprecedented milestone in mortgage banking history." Key to the new era of the housing Ponzi scheme was the reduction of capital required to back up the unsavory mortgages as the Countrywide press release clearly stated: "The strategic agreement contemplates efforts by Fannie Mae and Countrywide to work together to create capital structures that reduce the intensive capital demands of mortgage banking. The Alternative Servicing Compensation mortgage-backed securities (ASC MBS) product developed by Fannie Mae and recently issued by Countrywide is an initial effort to provide this flexibility."

Three months later, on October 7, 1999, *American Banker* reported that the newly liberated Countrywide was off to the subprime races: "Countrywide's monthly report underscored a shift in strategy throughout the mortgage industry.

Now that the refinancing boom has ended, lenders are making more loans to people who previously might not have
qualified for a mortgage." The article went on to mention
the comments of Salomon Smith Barney analyst Thomas
O'Donnell over "Fannie Mae's official entrance into the sector last week, when it launched a program aimed at providing lower-cost mortgages for people with slightly impaired
credit, would spur interest in serving the sector and provide
liquidity to help lending increase their subprime business."

After the banking meltdown, the SEC would file a civil
suit against Mozilo's and Countrywide's many violations,
but Johnson and Raines avoided such accountability for the
crash. Johnson, a consummate survivor, is the man who
started Fannie Mae on its mortgage derivatives spree during
the 1990s, after he had served as a managing director for corporate finance at Lehman Brothers, and who, after retiring
from Fannie Mae, went on to be a director of Goldman
Sachs. It is true that Johnson had begun as an aide to Democratic senator and later presidential aspirant Walter Mondale and throughout his private and public career had
identified with liberal rhetoric while personally enriching
himself with hundreds of millions of dollars in stock options, salary, retirement packages, and other compensation.

His protégé and successor at Fannie Mae would provide
an even more egregious example of a liberal veneer covering
a rapacious capitalist greed. If you were to pick a spokesman
for the American dream, it must have occurred to his backers

in the Clinton administration that Franklin Delano Raines was a pretty damn good one. Saddled by his father with a rather heavyweight name—sharing those fulsome first five syllables with the renowned president—the African American Raines's rise through Harvard and into high posts in successive Democratic administrations was stunning in a nation far more race- and class-bound than it likes to imagine.

After earning big bucks on Wall Street while his party was in the political wilderness during the Reagan era, Raines built a reputation as a skilled negotiator and clear-headed adviser while working in the Clinton White House as head of the large Office of Management and Budget. But it was when he again passed through the revolving door of the federal government to return to Fannie Mae to become the director of the nation's largest buyer of home mortgages that he fully realized his potential as an icon, a mustachioed Horatio Alger stereotype proving the famed American elevator could still raise one to the top in a single lifetime.

The *New York Times*' Richard Stevenson wrote on May 17, 1998, that Raines saw his father take five years building a home with his own hands. "To have such an emotional connection to a home may serve Mr. Raines well as he leaves his post this week as White House budget chief to take over Fannie Mae, the curious and huge Washington corporation whose government-mandated mission is to encourage homeownership, especially among low-and moderate-income working people."

Fannie Mae and its smaller, parallel organizations such as Freddie Mac are often described the way the *Times* does here, because they were spawned by the government and have implicit advantages—on taxes and interest rates—and implied backing from the federal government. However, although they were originally chartered by it during the Depression, Fannie Mae and siblings have not been part of the government since 1968. When they profit, as they did enormously before the recession, the dividends go to shareholders and the bonuses to executives. In no sense are they independent government agencies like the Social Security Administration, depending on a form of taxation to be redistributed as a social safety net. And while they have a vague legacy and "mission" to broaden the base of home ownership in the United States—and pay lip service to this in their periodic presentations on Capitol Hill—their prime agenda is to produce profit.

Certainly, Raines, all heartwarming stories aside, was a corporate CEO, not a director of a social service agency—and he certainly wasn't compensated like one, being paid, for example, the second-highest compensation package in the mortgage business in 2001: $4 million in salary and an estimated $10 million in stock options. (The CEO of Freddie Mac was third, with numbers nearly as staggering, according to *National Mortgage News*, May 6, 2002.)

And like most modern CEOs, Raines was far more focused on short-term gain than on long-term goals. Thus, although his six-year reign at Fannie Mae was successful in generating huge profits, it also saw systemic accounting troubles—some called it fraud—that would force Raines to return some of his huge pay package, as well as a conveniently shortsighted view of the housing market as bubble-proof.

"We don't think that there is a housing bubble in the country," he told *Black Enterprise* magazine for an extensive profile in the May 2003 issue. Crediting low interest rates, he added, incorrectly, "People's incomes are higher so they can afford more housing and, obviously, the owners of the house [will] try to raise the price when they're selling it."

In fact, as was clear even then, real income for the vast majority of Americans—and especially those served by Raines's "American Dream Initiative" program—had been barely rising throughout the Clinton bubble. What everybody and his sister knew was that, in fact, folks who would have never qualified for loans based on income were for some reason being sought after by lenders, and that folks who did own their homes were leveraging their reassessed assets to buy second, third, or fourth places to "flip" in the red-hot market.

With credit so loose and the market booming, Raines and Fannie were sitting pretty. From *Black Enterprise*:

> Franklin D. Raines has a lot to smile about. In mid-January, the Federal Mortgage Loan Association, better known as Fannie Mae, accomplished something that's rather uncommon these days—increased profits.

> Operating net income for fiscal 2002 rose 19.1% to
> $6.4 billion, or $6.31 on $10.6 billion in net interest in-
> come. And while Wall Street remains jittery after a
> slew of corporate scandals, economic uncertainty, and
> whispers of housing bubbles, Fannie Mae's 54-year-old
> chief executive is at the helm of a financial products
> and services giant that posted its 16th consecutive year
> of double-digit earnings growth.

Sure, Raines wasn't above exploiting Fannie's high-
minded charter to brush back critics, like the *Wall Street Journal*, who have long been nearly obsessive in pointing out that
the GSEs enjoyed unfair advantages because of their historic
government ties. From the *Wall Street Journal*: "The point all
of this makes, and the point we've been trying to make all
along, is that Fan and Fred don't function like other companies. The two biggest mortgage holders in the country are
allowed to pile up debt, implicitly guaranteed by taxpayers,
without being held to even the minimum of corporate gov-
ernance standards that every other publicly traded company
has to observe. Sooner or later this is asking for trouble."

That "trouble" was detailed by the *New York Times*'
Gretchen Morgenson in her September 5, 2009, story com-
memorating the one-year anniversary of the $200 billion in
bailout funds "to keep Fannie in the black." Morgenson reported on efforts of Florida Democratic congressman Alan
Grayson to expose the malpractices of Fannie Mae's Raines

and other executives. Grayson was livid that in addition to the government's having to take over the mortgage giant, taxpayers then had to foot the legal bills for Raines ($2.43 million) and two other Fannie Mae execs (another $3.87 million) for just ten months ending in July 2009, with the tab continuing to rise. The legal expenses were generated from shareholder lawsuits.

The reporter reminded readers, "With all the turmoil of the financial crisis, you may have forgotten about the book-cooking that went on at Fannie Mae. Government inquiries found that between 1998 and 2004, senior executives at Fannie manipulated its results to hit earnings targets and generate $115 million in bonus compensation. Fannie had to restate results by $6.3 billion."

In other words, the books were "cooked" so Raines and his pals—chief financial officer J. Timothy Howard and former controller Leanne Spencer—could earn bonuses based on the successes suggested by those phony figures. The government sought through litigation to collect from the three $100 million in fines and $115 million in restitution for the unearned bonuses—$84.6 million from Raines alone—but settled for $31.4 million from the three. As part of the settlement, Raines, Howard, and Spencer did not have to admit wrongdoing.

None of this sat very well with Congressman Grayson, who told Morgenson: "I cannot see the justification of people who led these organizations into insolvency getting a free ride. It goes right to the heart of what people find most disturbing in this situation—the absolute lack of justice." He asked, "When did Uncle Sam become Uncle Sap?" and seemed to be speaking for all taxpayers when he lamented: "It is wrong in a very deep sense. The essence of our society is that people who do good things are rewarded and people who do bad things are punished. Where is the punishment for Raines, Howard and Spencer? There is none."

Back in 2003, while bad things were certainly happening at Fannie Mae on his watch, Raines was showing a talent for obfuscation. As he assured *Black Enterprise* reporter Aisha Jefferson, "The *Wall Street Journal* finds problems where no other paper seems to find problems. They don't believe in intervening in the market to help housing and homeownership. And so, I think this is an effort to make the case that Fannie Mae shouldn't exist."

Unfortunately, this was just a smokescreen. Fannie Mae actually was receiving pressure not from liberal politicians to become more heavily involved in riskier mortgages but from—what else?—the profit motive. With giants like Citi moving heavily into mortgage-based securities—a sector pioneered by Fannie itself—and increasingly betting on riskier and riskier loans, the GSEs were actually playing catch-up. And when they decided to push their chips deep into the hottest, yet most unpredictable, Alt-A and subprime mortgages, it was not at the behest of the Barney Franks of this world but rather in pursuit of Wall Street profits.

That sorry reality, brought home by the spectacular crash of 2008, was clearly outlined in testimony that Armando Falcon offered two years after the government fully took control of Fannie and Freddie. In his testimony before the bipartisan Financial Crisis Inquiry Commission, which Congress had created to analyze the causes of the banking meltdown, the former chief regulator of the housing agencies did not mince words.

Falcon corrected the errors of Democrats and Republicans in assigning responsibility. The problem, he stated, with the so-called government-sponsored but essentially private institutions that the conservatives are so happy to vilify and that liberals feel the need to defend is that they represented the worst of both worlds. Although originally chartered by the government, they had morphed into super for-profit monstrosities run by executives whose huge bonuses depended on the price of the company stock. As Falcon put it in his testimony: "Ultimately the companies were not unwitting victims of an economic down cycle or flawed products and services of theirs. Their failure was deeply rooted in a culture of arrogance and greed."

In short, they behaved like the other financial conglomerates, but the government-sponsored housing enterprises were protected by powerful members of Congress and what turned out to be a strong guarantee that the taxpayers would cover their bad paper.

They do deserve considerable blame for the banking disaster that ensued, and while it is hardly the whole story, it gave the free-market conservatives a convenient target. But it also presents them with a contradiction that they refuse to confront. The housing enterprises failed not because they were do-gooder public entities but because they weren't. Their top executives were driven by the same desire for outlandish profit that their counterparts at AIG and Citigroup had. As Falcon put it, referring to then Fannie Mae CEO Franklin Raines: "While all of this political power satisfied the egos of Fannie and Freddie executives, it ultimately served one primary purpose: the speedy accumulation of personal wealth by any means . . . In the case of CEO Franklin Raines, he collected over $90 million in total compensation from 1998 to 2003. Of that amount, $52 million was directly tied to achieving earnings-per-share goals. However, the earnings goal turned out to be unachievable without breaking rules and hiding risks."

It only adds insult to injury to blame the unfettered greed of folks like Raines, and his congressional allies who were lavishly attended to by those agencies, on a concern for the low-income homebuyers who were their main victims.

CHAPTER 8

Goldman Cleans Up

"The first sound they'll hear is their heads hitting the floor," Treasury Secretary Henry M. Paulson Jr. informed President George W. Bush with undisguised glee. It was in the Oval Office on the morning of September 4, 2008, and Paulson was telling the president, as he recounts in his memoir, *On the Brink*, that the government was set to seize the housing giants Fannie Mae and Freddie Mac. "Mr. President, we're going to move quickly and take them by surprise."

That was two months before the presidential election that would propel Barack Obama into the White House, and the news the night before was that Sarah Palin had electrified the Republican convention with her acceptance of the vice presidential nomination. For the Republicans, faced with a collapsing economy, the crash of the ostensibly government-sponsored housing agencies provided a convenient target. This was not Lehman Brothers, the venerable Wall Street investment bank Paulson would let slip into bankruptcy eleven days later, or one of the other major banks like Goldman Sachs, Paulson's alma mater, which would require tens of billions of dollars in government bailout funds to survive.

Goldman had invested heavily in the derivatives that were now deemed toxic, playing both ends of the market while investors had suffered. But for Paulson, it was convenient to divert attention from the company he had run to those considered more directly connected with the government. As we saw in the last chapter, that is a difference without much meaning, as Goldman, just like Fannie Mae and Freddie Mac, traded on the stock market, was driven by the lust for exorbitant profit, and was a partner in what should have been a crime in hustling suspect derivatives. The derivatives that Goldman and the other banks sold and packaged contained many of the mortgages that the Government Sponsored Enterprises (GSEs) had backed and securitized.

No doubt Goldman Sachs had more power over government decisions than did Fannie Mae and Freddie Mac, the official GSEs. Proof of that came when Goldman was allowed to convert overnight into a bank holding company to qualify for TARP funds and other desperately needed federal assistance but otherwise was allowed to keep its leadership intact. Not so the folks at the GSEs, who were summarily fired for their comparable sins.

Speaking of Bush, Paulson would write in his memoir: "Like him, I am a firm believer in free markets, and I certainly hadn't come to Washington planning to do anything to inject the government into the private sector. But Fannie and Freddie were congressionally charted companies that already relied heavily on implicit government support."

That's the saving rationale that allowed these free-marketers to justify the largest nationalization of a privately owned entity in U.S. history. The takeover of these mammoth shareholder-owned companies without compensation could more properly be viewed as a brazen socialist seizure. In one fell swoop, the companies that owned or guaranteed $5 trillion of the nation's residential mortgages, one half the total, were now directly owned by the government. The American dream of privately owned housing, the family's castle, was, with that decision, turned over to the Washington bureaucracy without any evident discomfort on the part of the free-market ideologues in charge.

Until Paulson arrived as secretary of the Treasury in July 2006, there does not seem to have been much awareness that the economy was in for serious trouble. Of course, Bush himself, a speculative businessman, knew well that markets could be unstable and had witnessed the ignominious demise of Enron, the company led by his friend and lead campaign donor, "Kenny Boy" Lay. In the beginning of

Bush's first term, WorldCom, Global Crossing, and the top accounting firm Arthur Andersen had also collapsed. But then there was 9/11 and the perfect distraction of a never-ending war on terror to keep a president's mind off domestic unpleasantness.

According to Paulson's account, the president seemed genuinely shocked to hear that more trouble might be brewing with those newfangled derivatives and a total lack of market regulation. That's the way Paulson tells it, but surely Bush must have known something was awry, given that Enron's rise and fall was based on just such financial gimmickry. Still, Paulson wrote that the president did seem genuinely perplexed when his new Treasury secretary gave his depressing presentation on the state of the economy at a Camp David retreat in August 2006, five weeks after Paulson had been appointed to his government post. Outlining his view that in "recent history, there is a disturbance in the capital markets every four to eight years," Paulson told Bush, referring to the savings and loan scandal, the blowup of the bond market, the Asia crisis, and the Russia debt default: "I was convinced we were due for another disruption. I detailed the big increase in the size of unregulated pools of capital such as hedge funds and private-equity funds, as well as the exponential growth of unregulated over-the-counter (OTC) derivatives like credit default swaps. All of this has allowed an enormous amount of leverage—and risk—to creep into the financial system."

Now he tells us, or I should say, he tells the president. The leverage and risk didn't just "creep" into the financial system but was rather a logical result of specific deregulatory moves for which Paulson's old company Goldman Sachs had lobbied. On the leveraging of debt issue, it was Paulson back in 2004 who specifically had urged the SEC to allow investment banks to increase the debt they were permitted to carry.

Not surprisingly when a seemingly perplexed President Bush then asked Paulson: "How did this happen?" Paulson felt awkward in responding, as he recalls: "It was a humbling question for someone from the financial sector to be asked—after all, we were the ones responsible." Mark that comment, for it represents an extremely rare admission of culpability by a Wall Street leader. But it is also starkly revealing that while the financial moguls were well aware that deep trouble lay ahead, the key officials in the government were clueless.

It is quite bizarre that despite all of the developing negative signs concerning the market, Paulson would write in his memoir, "It was evident that the administration had not focused on these areas before, so I gave a quick primer on hedging, how and why it is done." Not, it should be noted, on credit default swaps and how they came to be totally unregulated, thanks in part to Bush's fellow Texan Phil Gramm and the legislation he pushed through the Senate with lame-duck president Clinton's blessing.

The level of ignorance on Bush's part is alarming, given that he had made much of his Harvard MBA and his own business experience in campaigning for the presidency. But Paulson in his memoir offers a rare admission of how shallow was the understanding also of the key bankers, like those at Goldman Sachs, who were trading in the suspect derivatives with such abandon. When the president asked what might trigger the big disruption of the market, Paulson mentioned "the lack of transparency of these CDS contracts (credit default swaps), coupled with their startling growth rate, unnerved me." But he added he didn't know what would cause the explosion because he seems to have been unaware even as late as August 2006 that it was subprime mortgages that were at the heart of the toxic packages.

"I misread the cause, and the scale, of the coming disaster," he admits. "Notably absent from my presentation was any mention of problems in housing or mortgages." In other words he claims to have been early in his concern about the toxic derivatives but was clueless as to what made them toxic.

As powerful as Paulson was, both as head of Goldman and then as U.S. Treasury secretary, he still did not understand the inner workings of the unregulated derivatives market that had made him a very rich man but would impoverish many others. "They took the money and ran" is the best way to describe the decade of irresponsible greed in which the top CEOs entrusted subordinates, claiming expertise in mathematical model building and market arbitrage, to do their wizardry, no questions asked. That story has been well documented in the case of the much-disgraced executives of Citigroup and AIG, but it remained for Paulson's memoir to confirm that the abysmal ignorance extended to the highest reaches of even mighty Goldman Sachs.

More startling is the fact that as Paulson moved to take over the U.S. Treasury Department he would bring with him the very same "experts" whose financial follies had risked Goldman's future. Paulson had been selected by Bush to run Treasury on the recommendation of the president's chief of staff, Joshua B. Bolton, a former director of the Office of Management and Budget and a Goldman executive. Nor was Paulson the first Goldman honcho to be named Treasury secretary, for Robert Rubin had provided exactly that precedent in the Clinton administration. But Paulson used the banking crisis as a justification for quickly putting Goldman employees and alums in charge of key outposts concerning the bailout.

Those close connections between the Treasury Department and his old firm—"Government Sachs"—were detailed in a *New York Times* story October 19, 2008, in which reporters Julie Creswell and Ben White cited in devastating detail examples of just how Goldman alums had come to control the government's bailout, which among other things benefited Goldman enormously: "It is a widely held view within the bank that no matter how much money you pile up, you are not a true Goldman star until you make your mark in the political sphere. While Goldman sees this as little more than giving back to the financial world, outside executives and analysts wonder about potential conflicts of interest presented by the firm's unique perch."

These outside observers were troubled by the fact that decisions Goldman alumni made at Treasury directly affected Goldman's fortunes. They also questioned why Goldman, whose flagrant use of "exotic securities" helped precipitate the crisis, now had such a leading role in trying to fix it. One of the strongest hands was that of Neel T. Kashkari, a thirty-five-year-old investment banker who was brought into the Treasury department in 2006 from Goldman's San Francisco office to head up the $700-billion banking bailout program. It was widely reported that Kashkari, who had been a financial adviser to technology companies while in San Francisco, had no discernible expertise concerning the issues at hand, and it seemed obvious that his main asset was his total loyalty to Paulson's vision of what needed to be accomplished. Kashkari in turn picked Reuben Jeffery III, another former Goldman executive, to serve as the chief investment officer.

The list goes on, but just to name a few, there was Dan Jester, another Goldman alum who played a key role in the takeover of Fannie Mae and Freddie Mac, and Steve Shafran, another trusted Paulson subordinate from Goldman, who was put in charge of money market policy.

After bailing out AIG, which listed Goldman as its top customer for the credit default swaps that were now of dubious worth, Paulson turned to Edward M. Liddy, a Goldman director, to become chair and CEO of the company in which the U.S. government was now the major owner. Liddy, another pretend innocent in all of these incestuous shenanigans, took heat for his defense of the $440,000 AIG executive retreat at a luxury resort in Monarch Beach, California, held on the heels of the taxpayer bailout. His actions now are defended as mistakes made by a well-intentioned outsider who decided to work for a dollar a year after Paulson appointed him head of AIG.

That is just garbage. Liddy was complicit in Goldman Sachs's role in creating this meltdown. As a director of Goldman Sachs, according to *Forbes*, he was paid $675,770 in stock in 2007 and would have come in for some questioning had the firm gone down; Liddy had sat on its audit committee during the five years before he resigned that seat to take over AIG in September 2008. As for his salary sacrifice, not to worry: In 2005, when he was still CEO and chair of Allstate Insurance, he received $26.7 million in compensation.

What we have here is a rare glimpse into the workings of the billionaires' club, that elite gang of perfectly legal loan sharks who in only the most egregious cases will be judged as criminals—Bernard Madoff, former chair of NASDAQ, comes to mind. These other amoral sharks, who confiscated billions from shareholders and the 401(k) accounts of innocent victims, were rewarded handsomely, rarely needing to break the laws their lobbyists had purchased.

The dealings between AIG and Goldman would later form the stuff of scandal, as it turned out that bailout money had been passed through AIG to pay back Goldman Sachs and other clients at full value for their questionable investments. That secret deal was brokered by Timothy Geithner, then head of the New York Fed, whose close ties to Goldman have been described.

Geithner was also criticized by former leaders of Lehman Brothers and others for having colluded with Paulson to allow that institution to descend into bankruptcy. The two men had jointly agreed to refuse Lehman's request to become a bank holding company and thereby qualify for federal bailout funds. Yet a week after Lehman's ignominious crash into bankruptcy, that very same privilege was extended to Goldman Sachs and JPMorgan Chase.

Paulson, even before becoming Bush's Treasury secretary and while still heading Goldman, had developed a close relationship with Geithner, who, as head of the New York Fed, would act in a manner that much benefitted Goldman and who would succeed Paulson in the new Obama administration as Treasury secretary. As Paulson wrote: "Tim Geithner, president of the Federal Reserve Bank of New York, shared my concern and pressed Wall Street firms hard to clean up their act while I was at Goldman. I had loaned him Gerry Corrigan, a Goldman managing director and risk expert who had been a no-nonsense predecessor of Tim's at the New York Fed."

Does it get any clubbier? Goldman was then, and even more so later, key to marketing the toxic derivatives that no one understood, so Paulson must have thought, "If they are having trouble over at the Fed figuring it out, why not send one of our guys back to straighten them out?" They never did figure it out, and Paulson, despite the concern he claims he expressed to Bush in August 2006, nine months later was downplaying any danger of a collapse in the subprime mortgage market. As he put it in April 2007: "I don't see [it] imposing a serious problem. I think it's going to be largely contained." And six months after that, in October 2007, Paulson once again insisted, "I can't think of any situation where the backdrop of the global economy was as healthy as it is today." He followed that rosy assessment with an even more optimistic one in May 2008, when all hell was obviously breaking loose: "The worst is likely to be behind us."

Months later, in September 2008, came his infamous three-page, take-it-or-leave-it proposal to Congress that the government fork over $700 billion in bailout funds, and he was successful in insisting that no strings be attached in the form of punishment for CEOs, oversight, or control on bonuses. As Democratic congressman Brad Sherman of California put it: "Basically they gave Congress a ransom note: 'We've got your 401(k) and if you want to see your 401(k) alive again, give us $700 billion in unmarked bills.'"

The threat worked, and the bailout intrusion into the ostensibly free market of a scope unprecedented in U.S. history passed by a wide margin in Congress, with few questions asked. It was, for better or worse, a bipartisan effort, not only in the approval of Congress for the overall payout but the close working relationship of the triumvirate that would actually run the wild ride of the bailout in 2008. Just as the trio of Rubin, Summers, and Greenspan had done under Clinton, now it would be a similar collection from the Fed and Treasury that would be in charge, secretively and no questions asked. As Paulson in his memoir describes the process of making huge decisions back then, often unbeknownst to the public and even Congress: "I believe the most important part of the story is the way Ben Bernanke, Tim Geithner, and I worked as a team through the worst financial crisis since the Great Depression. There can't be many other examples of economic leaders managing a crisis who had as much trust in one another as we did."

Trust is good, but nothing in his memoir indicates that there were any of the checks and balances that should have also been at work, given that they represented three institutions with very different areas of responsibility. Particularly troubling is the relationship between Geithner, who as head of the New York Fed had prime responsibility for monitoring companies like Goldman Sachs, and Paulson, that company's former chair who was now supposedly, through the president, representing the national interest more broadly.

On the contrary Paulson and Geithner, in the scamming to save failing institutions from Bear Stearns to AIG, shared the assumption that the survival of major investment houses, particularly Goldman Sachs and Morgan Stanley, was essential to the survival of the American economy. Lehman Brothers had been treated as exceptional because of the particular structuring of its portfolio problems, but others could not be allowed to follow the Lehman downfall, for which Paulson was being strongly criticized by many of his powerful Wall Street friends.

Geithner, too, later came under criticism for the bailouts, as detailed in an April 27, 2009, *New York Times* story describing his role in the bank rescue as "a leading architect of those bailouts, the activist at the head of the pack." The story cites discontent by bankers that there were "too many intrusive strings" to the rescue, while "a range of critics—lawmakers, economists and even former Federal Reserve colleagues— say that the bailout Mr. Geithner has played such a central role in fashioning is overly generous to the financial industry at taxpayer expense."

The story, whose headline referred to him as "Member and Overseer of Finance Club" and written by Jo Becker and Gretchen Morgenson, noted: "An examination of Mr. Geithner's five years as president of the New York Fed, an era of unbridled and ultimately disastrous risk-taking by the financial industry, shows that he forged unusually close relationships with executives of Wall Street's giant financial institutions . . . His actions, as a regulator and later a bailout king, often aligned with the industry's interests and desires, according to interviews with financiers, regulators and analysts and a review of Federal Reserve records."

This is not surprising, as Geithner's appointment calendars from 2007 and 2008 reveal private social and business meals and meetings with top executives of Goldman Sachs, Citibank, JPMorgan Chase, and Morgan Stanley. The *Times* detailed the atmosphere in the high echelons of the New York Fed's world and how Geithner fit in:

> The New York Fed is, by custom and design, clubby and opaque. It is charged with curbing banks' risky impulses, yet its president is selected by and reports to a board dominated by the chief executives of some of those same banks. Traditionally, the New York Fed president's intelligence gathering role has involved routine consultation with financiers, though Mr. Geithner's recent predecessors generally did not meet with them unless senior aides were also present, according to the bank's former general counsel.
>
> By those standards, Mr. Geithner's reliance on bankers, hedge fund managers and others to assess the market's health—and provide guidance once it faltered—stood out.

The framework during the time Geithner worked on the "team" with Paulson and Ben Bernanke to manage the crisis was "all Wall Street all the time," with the clear assumption being that what was good for big finance was good for America, and vice versa. Main Street didn't quite see it that way, and as vice presidential candidate Sarah Palin curtly informed Paulson, as he recalled in his memoir, "Hank, the American people don't like bailouts." She was right of course, but Paulson was able to wield a mesmerizing argument that had the virtue of corresponding to the reality of the grotesquely distorted U.S. and world financial structure: The casino was not a refuge from the real world; it *was* the real world. The paper money games of "The Street" trumped the realities of hard work and savings of the rest of the population, so much so that as Paulson explains in his memoir, he felt the need to shape the debate of an ongoing presidential campaign by telling both Barack Obama and John McCain how to treat the crisis in their remarks, and while McCain grumbled, they both went along.

The great exercise in political democracy turned into a charade in its treatment of the overwhelming issue of the day, the economic crisis, with the candidates parroting the words of the secretary of the Treasury planted to assure the moguls of Wall Street, no matter how unsatisfactory it might seem to ordinary voters. It was everything the agrarian-based Jeffersonian democrats had most feared in the way of concentrated national power.

Even the sitting president was, as Paulson captures his role, a helpless figure plaintively questioning how we got into this but having to go along with whatever the Wall Street–savvy Treasury secretary told him had to be done. "'How did we get to this point?' the president asked in frustration." Paulson recalls, referring to his request to Bush that they come up with an $85-billion guarantee for AIG, which was at that moment in free fall. "He wanted to understand how we couldn't let a financial institution fail without inflicting widespread damage on the economy," Paulson states. But what he told the president was beside the point of that very relevant question.

The proper answer is that extreme and obviously stupid antiregulatory policies had permitted the unwieldy and bizarrely managed AIG, once a staid and rigorously regulated insurance company, to become a sprawling, totally out-of-control conglomerate with its fingers in more pots than anyone could count or was aware of. It was indeed too big to fail, and the taxpayers would be left on the hook in a stunning repudiation of the Reagan Revolution, which the first President Bush had properly dismissed as "voodoo economics." Instead, Paulson spoke gibberish to the president, who bought it:

> I explained that AIG differed from Lehman, because Lehman had issues with both capital and liquidity, whereas AIG just had a liquidity problem. The investment bank had been loaded with toxic assets worth far less than the value at which they were carried, creating a capital hole. Nervous counterparties had fled, draining liquidity.
>
> In AIG's case the problem wasn't capital—at least we didn't think so at the time. The insurer held many toxic mortgages, but its most pressing problem was a

derivative portfolio that included a large amount of credit default swaps on residential mortgage CDOs. The decline in housing values, and now the cuts in AIG's ratings, required it to post more collateral. Suddenly, AIG owed money seemingly everywhere, and it was scrambling to come up with $85 billion on short notice. "If we don't shore up AIG," I said, "we will likely lose several more financial institutions. Morgan Stanley, for one."

I noted that an AIG collapse would be much more devastating than the Lehman failure because of its size and the damage it would do to millions of individuals whose retirement accounts it insured.

What he did not tell the president but makes clear in his memoir is that the firm Paulson had recently headed, Goldman Sachs, was right up there with Morgan Stanley at the top of the list of financial firms that could collapse. Indeed, Goldman had the largest account of toxic derivatives ostensibly insured by AIG. He was also dead wrong in saying the problem was one of liquidity alone and not capital, since AIG lacked the capital reserves to back up the massive credit default swap insurance agreements it had sold. Paulson made sure in the AIG bailout that Goldman got back every penny it thought it was owed.

But the fuller answer to the president's question of "How did we get to this point?" lies in a more accurate comparison of the Lehman plight with that of AIG. Those who argue that it was not the fault of the deregulation craze of the 1990s, as does Bill Clinton, who signed off on the legislation that gutted Glass-Steagall, refer often to the Lehman example to make their point. They note correctly that Lehman did not require deregulation to be what it was, still primarily an investment house. But they never offer the obvious conclusion: Because it was not too big to fail and had not become a sprawling monstrosity of the likes of AIG and Citigroup, it was allowed to fail without the entire economy being destroyed. The example of the latter two is precisely the opposite: They had to be saved because they had been allowed to grow in ways potentially destructive of the entire economic structure.

And if he really wanted to educate the president he served, and the Democratic one who came before him, Paulson should have pointed out that the reason he, one of the nation's leading investment bankers as well as the Treasury secretary, was so in the dark as to what was going on is that he didn't really have a grasp on what his old company or AIG actually owned. Those credit default swaps and the collateralized debt obligations they pretended to cover had developed into the biggest financial bubble in human history because of the law pushed by Republican Phil Gramm and signed by Democratic president Bill Clinton to the cheers of Wall Street lobbyists, including most prominently those representing Goldman Sachs, that categorically freed all such financial packages from any regulatory supervision.

But Paulson didn't tell the bewildered president anything of the sort. Instead, he asked for and received a blank check, no strings attached, to save AIG and Citigroup from bankruptcy. Give the president credit for not buying the argument, even as he went along feeling he had no choice. And when the president still said he didn't get it, Ben Bernanke, the head of the Federal Reserve, who was also in attendance for that White House emergency meeting, chimed in with support for Paulson's incredulous cause. As Paulson recalls: "The president found it hard to believe that an insurance company could be so systemically important. I tried to explain that AIG was an unregulated holding company comprising many highly regulated insurance entities. Ben chimed in with a pointed description: 'It's like a hedge fund sitting on top of an insurance company.'"

But why was an unregulated hedge fund allowed to sit on top of an insurance company? As President Bush told Paulson and Bernanke after being bullied into going along with the massive AIG bailout: "Someday you guys are going to have to tell me how we ended up with a system like this and what we need to do to fix it."

That's the fundamental question that Obama had raised back in the early months of his primary campaign, when at Cooper Union he had forthrightly challenged the wisdom of the radical deregulation of the Clinton years. But now that the meltdown was under way in earnest, and Paulson and Geithner were getting to directly influence the speeches of the candidates, the subject would be avoided. Those seeking to replace Bush as president were now sinking into the quagmire of Wall Street's perverse take on reality, which in the end would make sense and serve the interests only of those who created the problem and not of the mass of people a president is sworn to serve.

CHAPTER 9

Sucking Up
to the Bankers:
Crisis Handoff from
Bush to Obama

An odd thing happened on the way to the 2008 presidential election: Both major party candidates embraced the very folks who had helped engineer the banking meltdown that was far and away the most important issue to voters. Republican candidate John McCain and his Democratic opponent, Barack Obama, each given to occasional populist rhetoric against Wall Street, nonetheless embraced its prevailing philosophy. Both scrambled to enlist not only the big-dollar contributions but also, more frighteningly, the "expertise" of those who had advocated the financial industry deregulations at the heart of this meltdown.

McCain appointed as his campaign cochair Phil Gramm, who went from being chair of the Senate Banking Committee, where he cosponsored the disastrous legislation that bore his name, to becoming a top executive at UBS Warburg, one of the banks that most egregiously exploited its loopholes.

But Gramm and the Republicans, as readers of this book now know in painful detail, couldn't have done it without the support of Clinton's key economic team. They would resurface when Obama turned for economic advice to Robert Rubin and his key protégés, Lawrence Summers and Timothy Geithner. The first big tip-off that Obama would turn to the Rubin crowd came in July 2008, when, even before securing the nomination, he appointed Jason Furman, who ran the Hamilton Project at the Brookings Institution, cofounded by Rubin, to be the Obama campaign's economic policy director. Furman hardly distinguished himself four years earlier in that same role in John Kerry's sputtering presidential campaign, which all but ignored the gathering economic storms.

After that failed campaign, Furman showed his ideological hand with a bold defense of a new vision of "progressive" economics based on the experience of the Clinton era. A paper he wrote in November 2005 for a panel for the Center for American Progress, entitled "Wal-Mart: A Progressive Success Story," argued the case for Clinton's triangulation by celebrating the example of employers like Wal-Mart, whose low prices benefitted consumers but whose workers survived thanks only to subsidies from the government-supported welfare-to-work programs of publicly funded expansions of Medicaid and earned income tax credits, which made those low wages less onerous. As Furman wrote:

> But Wal-Mart, like other retailers and employers of less-skilled workers, does not pay enough for a family to live the dignified life Americans have come to expect and demand. That is where a second progressive success story comes in: the transformation of our social safety net from a support for the indigent to a system . . . that makes work pay. In the 1990s, President Clinton fought for expansions in support for low-income workers, including a more generous Earned Income Tax Credit (EITC) and efforts to ensure that children did not lose their Medicaid if their parents took a low-paid job. The bulk of the benefits of these expansions go to the workers that receive them, not to the corporations that employ them.

This may be an ingenious argument in defense of Wal-Mart's profits abetted by Clinton's economic policy, but it should have been a clue to Obama's own views that the community organizer would pick the author of that rationalization to run the economic side of his campaign. It is trickle-down economics of the sort that would guide the banking bailout: Serve Wall Street a banquet, and hope the crumbs fall to distressed homeowners and the jobless. The die was cast in the weeks after his election, when Obama made it clear that he would not only appoint others from Robert Rubin's team but also endorse an expansion of the enormously costly bailout of Citigroup.

As previously noted, this bailout involved $50 billion of taxpayer money thrown at Citigroup and the guarantee of $306 billion for the bank's toxic securities that would have been illegal if not for changes in the law that Citigroup secured with the decisive help of Rubin and Summers. Yet despite that dismal record of dismantling sound regulation, Obama picked Summers to be director of his National Economic Council and Geithner as the new Treasury secretary, with Furman chosen as Summers' deputy director.

Geithner, thanks to the strong recommendation of Rubin and Summers, his bosses at Treasury during the Clinton years, had been appointed chair of the New York Federal Reserve Bank, where he was the main government official charged with regulating Citigroup, a task at which he obviously failed. Yet at one secret weekend meeting at the New York Fed, it was Geithner who hammered out the Citigroup bailout deal with Treasury secretary Henry Paulson and a very actively involved Rubin. It was an appointment that former Citigroup chair Sandy Weill clearly approved of, describing Geithner more as a possible patsy than as a regulator for his bank's activities: "He had a baby face," Weill recalled in an interview with the *New York Times'* Jo Becker and Gretchen Morgenson published on April 26, 2009. "He didn't have a lot of experience in dealing with the industry."

Quite a recommendation for someone pushed by Rubin, who was then working for Weill at Citigroup, to be the Fed's main overseer of Citigroup's activities. Geithner was forty-two when he took the helm of the most influential of the twelve regional banks in the Federal Reserve system, with astounding reach and power over the U.S. economy.

The selection of Geithner, a pro–Wall Street Clinton veteran, assured that the New York Fed—the main regulatory agency over Wall Street—would guarantee that Citigroup's interests were attended to. And Citigroup's influence would extend throughout the Bush years and into the next administration, thanks to Rubin's connections with Obama. The *Washington Post*'s David Cho and Neil Irwin reported on November 25, 2008, just after Obama's election, that Bush's Treasury secretary, Henry M. Paulson Jr., had planned no further bailouts before the new administration took office—that is, until "Rubin, an old colleague from Goldman Sachs, told Paulson in phone calls that the government had to act, according to industry sources familiar with their discussions." The reporters, citing anonymous sources, wrote that in the closing days before the bailout was negotiated, "Rubin called Paulson several times to make the case for intervention on behalf of Citigroup and the banking system as a whole."

This outrageous conflict of interest in which Rubin gets to exploit his ties to both the outgoing and the incoming administrations was best described by *Washington Post* writer Steven Pearlstein on November 25, 2008: "The ultimate irony is that just as Rubin & Co. were being bailed out at Citi by the Bush administration, President-elect Obama was announcing a new economic team drawn almost entirely from Rubin's acolytes."

Instead of the far tougher deal previously negotiated on the bailout of AIG, the arrangement with Citigroup left the executives, including Rubin, who brought Citigroup to the brink of ruin still in charge. Nor was there any guarantee of the value of the mortgage bundles that taxpayers would be on the line for. That is because, as candidate Obama clearly stated in his major economics address back in March 2008, the deregulation pushed though during the Clinton years ended transparency in banking.

After the inauguration, the new Obama administration made it clear from day one that pleasing Wall Street rather than distraught homeowners would be the focal point of policy. On February 10, 2009, new Treasury secretary Geithner, rising to what he termed "a challenge more complex than any our financial system has ever faced," committed to give up to $2 trillion more to the very folks who profited from that malignant complexity. For all the brave talk about transparency and accountability in the banking bailout, he gave the swindlers who got us into this mess yet another blank check to buy up the "toxic assets" they gleefully created.

According to the Congressional Oversight Panel created by Congress to monitor the bailout, the Bush Treasury Department had already overpaid by $78 billion of our money in the first ten purchases of those assets. Yet Geithner insisted that "Congress acted quickly and courageously" in throwing that money at Wall Street without requiring any accountability. At the same time, there was still no commitment to directly help the millions of homeowners already foreclosed out of their homes, with millions more to come.

The *New York Times* report of February 10, 2009, on the Geithner plan got it right. While acknowledging its "boldness," the *Times* noted that "the plan largely repeats the Bush administration's approach of deferring to many of the same companies and executives who had peddled risky loans and investments at the heart of the crisis and failed to foresee many of the problems plaguing the markets." Apparently Geithner and White House economic czar Lawrence Summers won out over David Axelrod and other Obama advisers more loyal to the wishes of grassroots voters. The *Times* noted that "as intended by Mr. Geithner, the plan stops short of intruding too significantly into bankers' affairs even as they come onto the public dole."

The word "dole" is usually applied pejoratively to welfare mothers sustained in their dire poverty by meager government handouts, not to top bankers ripping off the taxpayers. But as opposed to welfare mothers, who must survive stringent monitoring, the bankers would be largely self-monitoring. Under Obama as with Bush and Clinton before him, there was to be tough love for welfare mothers but never for bankers.

It is true that Obama in his first months in office launched a stimulus package that brought some small measure of help to Main Street but which was the subject of much Congressional debate and strident Republican opposition. The problem was not with the quite reasonable and, if anything, underfunded stimulus package. The problem lay with what was not being debated: the far more expensive Wall Street bailouts that were pushed through by both Bush and Obama, largely in secret, in hurried deal making primarily by the unelected secretary of the Treasury and the chair of the Federal Reserve Bank.

In the fall of 2008, while Bush was still president, taxpayers began bailing out AIG with more than $140 billion, and then it went and lost $61.7 billion in the fourth quarter, more than any other company in history had ever lost in one quarter. Now in 2009, Obama was president, and it was on his watch that government officials huddled late into the first weekend of March and decided to reward AIG for its startling failure with thirty billion more of our dollars. Plus, they sweetened the deal by letting AIG off the hook for interest it had been obligated to pay on the money taxpayers previously gave the company. That's money, as it turned out, that was passed on to Goldman Sachs and other financial giants that had hedged their bets with what would have proved to be AIG's worthless credit default swaps, had U.S. taxpayers not been forced by their government to come to the rescue.

The Wall Street bailouts were a frantic response to a crisis that resulted from the radical deregulation pushed by former Goldman Sachs honcho Robert Rubin when he was President Clinton's Treasury secretary. Another Goldman Sachs chair-turned-Treasury-secretary, Henry Paulson, in the Bush administration, designed what became the more than $1-trillion bank bailout that will go down as the greatest swindle in U.S. history.

As we know, it was because of Paulson that AIG was saved from bankruptcy hours after Goldman rival Lehman Brothers was allowed to go down the drain. Why that reversal of strategy in a top-secret meeting called by then New York Fed chair Geithner? Why was Goldman's Lloyd Blankfein the only financial industry CEO in attendance? When that news leaked out, his role was defended as that of a noninvolved concerned citizen with expert knowledge, whose firm had no direct monetary stake in the outcome. That was a lie. Goldman Sachs was into AIG insurance policies for at least $20 billion.

Goldman Sachs alums were no less prominent in the Obama administration than had been the case with his Republican predecessor. A key example of the enduring influence of one firm would be on display in March 2009, when Obama picked former Goldman partner Gary Gensler for the position as head of the Commodity Futures Trading Commission, the position once held by Brooksley Born, the stalwart consumer watchdog back in the Clinton years who had stood for regulation of the derivatives that would humble the world's economy. Gensler was confirmed but only after jumping over a hurdle constructed by Bernie Sanders, the senator from Vermont, an independent in spirit as well as party label. Sanders placed Gensler's nomination on hold. Sounds like a minor issue to get worked up about, but the senator was right.

Gensler helped create this financial crisis when he was pushing for deregulation in the Treasury Department back in the Clinton era, when bipartisan cooperation with Wall Street lobbyists was all the rage. Sanders got right to the point: "While Mr. Gensler is clearly an intelligent and knowledgeable person, I cannot support his nomination. Mr. Gensler worked with Sen. Phil Gramm and Alan Greenspan to exempt credit default swaps from regulation, which led to the collapse of AIG and has resulted in the largest taxpayer bailout in U.S. history."

Sanders's hold did not stop the Gensler nomination because Congress and the president sought to give Wall Street whatever it wanted to make the stock market go up. And Gensler was a reassuring figure to the moguls of finance: a partner at Goldman Sachs before being brought by Goldman

exec Robert Rubin to the Treasury Department and promoted to Treasury undersecretary by Rubin's successor
Summers.

Back then in 1999, in congressional testimony before the
House Subcommittee on Risk Management, Research, and
Specialty Crops, Undersecretary Gensler supported the radical deregulation of the financial derivatives market, insisting
with great enthusiasm: "OTC derivatives directly and indirectly support higher investment and growth in living standards in the United States and around the world." These
exact words were uttered by Larry Summers in testimony
before another congressional committee almost a year earlier, when he warned of dire consequences should these markets be regulated. As to the many trillions of dollars in credit
swaps that now afflict the world economy, Gensler specifically called for freeing swaps of this kind from existing government regulation in the Commodity Exchange Act, which
regulated other futures such as wheat sales, testifying, "swap
transactions should not be regulated under the CEA."

His key argument, and that of his then boss, Summers, as
well, was that even raising the prospect of regulating what
have proved to be toxic derivatives would deny these financial instruments the "legal certainty" they needed to thrive.
What a loss that would be, warned Summers, who called the
financial derivatives market "a powerful symbol of the kind
of innovation and technology that has made the American
financial system as strong as it is today."

Gensler was just one of many Goldman alums that Obama brought into his administration despite the ongoing interests that their old firm had in the resolution of the banking mess. Another was Goldman's Washington lobbyist Mark Patterson, who in the first weeks of the new administration was hired to the key position of chief of staff to Geithner. The appointment clearly violated a rule that Obama had put into place when he assumed office, which barred the hiring of lobbyists from working on issues about which they had lobbied, but the rule was waived for Patterson, who had represented Goldman Sachs for the previous three years. He was named to the post the same day that Geithner began his first full day of work at Treasury by announcing rules limiting the role of lobbyists in the distribution of $350 billion in TARP funds.

Key to that drama was the costliest bailout ever, that of AIG, described in the previous chapter—AIG, whose credit default swaps backing the now plummeting housing-based derivatives turned out to have been backed by nothing more than a promise of repayment without capital reserves to back up that promise. Goldman Sachs turned out to be the main beneficiary of the government's AIG bailout.

As Treasury secretary, Geithner would be confronted by new revelations of his role in the AIG bailout, in which he betrayed the taxpayers who were footing the bill.

What had been hidden from public view was the fact that Geithner, as head of the New York Fed overseeing the AIG bailout, had pressured AIG not to reveal the names of the insured clients that it was paying with government funds. And it turned out that the New York Fed had also brokered a deal in which AIG paid out generously at full value of the losses that the insured companies, particularly Goldman, claimed.

Goldman Sachs originally packaged those derivatives with an expectation of their failure and, indeed, placed counter bets that ensured even higher profit on the downturn that left tens of millions throughout the world destitute when the housing bubble collapsed. As the *New York Times* editorialized in "Betting Against All of Us" on December 28, 2009: "During the bubble, Goldman Sachs and other financial firms created complicated mortgage-related investments, sold them to clients and then placed bets that those investments would decline in value." The practice, detailed in the *Times* by Gretchen Morgenson and Louise Story, allowed Wall Street to profit handsomely as its clients tanked. It also exemplified the financial meltdown, spreading the losses to pretty much everyone: "These deals are now the targets of various government and industry-led investigations. It may turn out that some or all of the products and practices were not illegal, in part because the derivatives at the heart of the transactions have been largely deregulated since 2000."

To summarize: That's the year that Clinton signed off on the Commodity Futures Modernization Act, discussed in the opening chapter, which former Goldman Sachs chair Rubin and his protégés pushed into law to deregulate those derivatives. And it was future Treasury secretary Paulson who headed up Goldman when it jumped through that legal loophole to package and sell those toxic derivatives. And it was this same Paulson as Treasury secretary in the administration of George W. Bush who along with then New York Fed chair Geithner pushed through the $180-billion rescue of AIG, the company that was holding the credit default swaps insuring the questionable Goldman derivatives.

Thus was launched the government's No Banker Left Behind program, begun by Paulson and continued by Geithner when Obama picked him to succeed Paulson. Within six months, the special inspector general in the Treasury Department would report that the bill had already run to nearly $3 trillion, an amount six times greater than would be spent by federal, state, and local governments the entire year on educating fifty million American children in elementary and secondary schools.

Where did the money go?

It took major pressure from a Congress reacting to an outraged public to discover that AIG, in addition to handing out hundreds of millions in bonuses to the very hustlers who created the firm's swindles, was a conduit for at least $70 billion in taxpayer money to reimburse the banks and stockbrokers who got us into this crisis with their bad bets.

No surprise there, given the incestuous world of finance. The revolving doors between the Treasury Department, the

Fed, and executive offices in the industry have been swinging throughout Republican and Democratic administrations. As a result, those orchestrating the bailout and those grabbing the money are for the most part friends and former colleagues, with enormous respect for each other but not for the American taxpayers and homeowners experiencing massive foreclosure rates.

Among the winners was Lawrence Summers, who remains convinced that he deserved every penny of the nearly $8 million that Wall Street firms paid him in 2008, when he was an Obama campaign adviser. And why shouldn't he be cut in on the loot from the loopholes in the derivatives market—many now toxic—that he pushed into law when he was Bill Clinton's Treasury secretary? No one has been more persistently effective in paving the way for the financial scams that enriched the titans of finance while impoverishing the rest of the world than the man who became the top economic adviser to President Obama.

It is especially disturbing that Summers got most of the $8 million or so from a major hedge fund at a time when such totally unregulated rich-guys-only investment clubs stand to make the most off the Obama administration's plan for saving the banks. The scheme, as announced by Treasury Secretary Geithner, is to clean up the toxic holdings of the banks using taxpayer money and then turn them over to hedge funds that will risk little of their own capital. At least the banks are somewhat government-regulated, which cannot be said of the hedge funds, thanks to Summers.

It was Summers, as much as anyone, who in the Clinton years prevented the regulation of the hedge funds that are at the center of the explosion of the derivatives bubble, and the fact that D. E. Shaw, a leading hedge fund, paid the Obama adviser $5.2 million in 2008 does suggest a serious conflict of interest. That sum is what Summers raked in for a part-time gig, in addition to the $2.77 million he received for forty speaking engagements, largely before banks and investment firms, and on top of the $586,996 he was paid as a professor and "president emeritus" at Harvard University.

Summers was then a top adviser to the Democratic presidential candidate, and that might have enhanced his lecture fees, which in 2008 averaged $69,425 per speaking engagement, the amount he received on each of two occasions when he appeared at JPMorgan Chase and Lehman Brothers before that latter company went bankrupt. Lehman had purchased a 20 percent stake in D. E. Shaw while Summers was employed by the hedge fund, and it would be interesting to know if the subject of the overlapping business came up during Summers' visit to Lehman.

Lehman was only one on an impressive list of top financial firms that consulted Summers during a troubled period. Goldman Sachs was so interested in his thoughts that it paid him $135,000 for one appearance, even though it soon needed $12 billion in taxpayer bailout funds. Citigroup, which has been going through hard times, managed only a $45,000 fee for a Summers rap. Merrill Lynch also could pony up only a scant $45,000 for a Summers appearance last November 12, 2008, but that was around the time when Merrill was in deep trouble, with the government arranging its sale. Summers, anticipating an appointment in the embarrassment the fee might bring, decided to turn over the $45,000 to a charity.

White House spokesperson Ben LaBolt told the *New York Times* that the compensation was not a conflict for Summers and indeed might be expected, since he was "widely recognized as one of the country's most distinguished economists."

But why was someone as compromised as Summers named the White House's point man overseeing trillions in federal commitments to the financial moguls he had enabled in creating this crisis, many of whom had benefitted him financially? Why would he be put in charge of the effort to create new regulations?

LaBolt emphasized to the *Wall Street Journal* that Summers "has been at the forefront of this administration's work . . . to put in place a regulatory framework that will strengthen the financial system and its oversight—all in an effort to help the families across America who have paid a very steep price for risky decisions made by Wall Street executives." Ah, those very same executives Summers had previously assured us could be trusted without any regulation. It is worth recalling in this context his previously cited testimony to a Senate panel in 1998, when, as deputy Treasury secretary, he spoke in opposition to Brooksley Born:

First, the parties to these kinds of contracts are largely
sophisticated financial institutions that would appear
to be eminently capable of protecting themselves
from fraud and counterparty insolvencies and most of
which are already subject to basic safety and soundness
regulation under existing banking and securities laws.
Second, given the nature of the underlying assets involved—namely, supplies of financial exchange and
other financial instruments—there would seem to be
little scope for market manipulation.

His efforts pushing deregulation back then would help
guarantee that today we would continue to be robbed big-
time, despite the change in party controlling the presidency
and Congress. This fear was confirmed in an April 2009
scathing report by the Treasury Department's special inspector general, Neil M. Barofsky, who charged that the TARP
program from its inception was designed to trust the Wall
Street recipients of the bailout funds to act responsibly on
their own, without accountability to the government that
gave them the money.

For all of its criticism of the original program, designed
by the Bush administration, the report was equally severe
in denouncing the Obama administration's plan to partner
with hedge funds and other private capital groups to buy
up the "toxic" holdings of the banks. Charging that the plan
carries "significant fraud risks," the inspector general's report

pointed out that almost all of the risk in this new trillion-dollar plan was being borne by the taxpayers. The so-called private investors would be able to put up money they borrowed from the Fed through "nonrecourse" loans, meaning if the toxic assets purchased proved too toxic and the scheme failed, the private investors could just walk away without repaying the Fed for those loans.

The reason those loans may prove even more toxic than expected and the price paid by this government-underwritten partnership far too high is that the government is purchasing the most suspect of the banks' mortgage packages. In addition, the plan is to accept at face value the evaluation of those packages by the very same credit-rating firms whose absurdly wrong estimates of the dollar worth of these securities helped create the problem that now haunts the world's economy.

"Arguably, the wholesale failure of the credit rating agencies to rate adequately such securities is at the heart of the securitization market collapse, if not the primary cause of the current credit crisis," the report found.

As with the entire banking bailout, the new Obama plan was likely to enrich the very folks who impoverished the rest of us, as the report notes: "The significant government-financed leverage presents a great incentive for collusion between the buyer and seller of the asset, or the buyer and other buyers, whereby, once again, the taxpayer takes a significant loss while others profit."

At the heart of this potentially massive fraud was the original decision of Treasury secretary Paulson to not require the recipients of the bailout, such as his old firm, Goldman Sachs, to account for how the money was spent. Unfortunately, President Obama's administration continued that practice. The only difference is that the amount of public money being put at risk was now far greater.

Geithner's close ties to the Wall Street elite was evidenced in a report in the *Wall Street Journal* on May 4, 2009, describing how the chair of the New York Federal Reserve Bank, Stephen Friedman, had made millions off his purchase of Goldman Sachs stock, a violation of Federal Reserve policy after Goldman—to qualify for government bailout funds— became a bank holding company. Geithner was then the New York Fed president, and he was complicit in approving that deal.

When Friedman bought stock in Goldman, the company he once headed and where he still was a director, he was hoping for a waiver of the stock ownership ban to permit him to hold his existing multimillion-dollar stock stash and to remain on the Goldman board. Geithner requested the waiver the previous October. Yet, without having received that waiver, Friedman went ahead in December and purchased 37,300 additional Goldman shares. With shares he added in January, a day after the waiver was granted, he ended up with 98,600 shares in Goldman Sachs, worth a total of $13,330,720 at the time of the *Wall Street Journal* report.

Friedman was in violation of the Fed's policy because, thanks in part to the urging of Geithner and the New York Fed, Goldman Sachs was allowed to become a bank holding company, making it eligible for government bailout funds (an option that Geithner had denied to Goldman rival Lehman Brothers). But that shift also put Goldman under more rigorous banking regulations that required Friedman, as Class C director of the New York Fed, a position in which he ostensibly represents the public instead of the banks that dominate the board, to step down as a Goldman director and divest his holdings. Instead, he stayed on the Goldman board and added additional shares while waiting for the Fed waiver. Nor did he inform the Federal Reserve of his additional purchases in December, and the lawyers for the New York Fed didn't know about that purchase until the *Journal* raised questions the following April. Friedman made a profit of about $3 million on the additional shares.

The significance of this conflict of interest was summarized by the lead of the *Journal* story: "The Federal Reserve Bank of New York shaped Washington's response to the financial crisis late last year, which buoyed Goldman Sachs Group Inc. and other Wall Street firms. Goldman received speedy approval to become a bank holding company in September and a $10 billion capital injection soon after."

As described in the previous chapter, Geithner as head of the New York Fed had worked closely with then Treasury secretary Paulson on the terms of the AIG bailout, which most handsomely benefitted Goldman Sachs, but that fact was kept from public view thanks to Geithner's insistence that the client list of AIG paid-off clients not be disclosed. The facts came out a year later, in November 2009, thanks to a devastating report by Special Inspector General Barofsky titled "Factors Affecting Efforts to Limit Payments to AIG Counterparties." The main factor was Geithner, who followed the lead of Goldman Sachs CEO Lloyd Blankfein in crowding the lifeboats with bankers.

Barofsky's report concluded that Geithner's scheme represented a "backdoor bailout" for the financial hustlers at the center of the market fiasco. Noting that Geithner denies that was his intention, the report states, "Irrespective of their stated intent, however, there is no question that the *effect* of [the New York Federal bank's] decisions—indeed, the very *design* of the federal assistance to AIG—was that tens of billions of dollars of government money was funneled inexorably and directly to AIG's counterparties."

Not surprisingly, a Treasury official defended the Fed's actions in not forcing "haircuts" on the full dollar-for-dollar payoff by AIG to the banks while Geithner was at the New York Fed: "The government could not unilaterally impose haircuts [lower prices] on creditors, and it would not have been appropriate for the government to pressure counterparties to accept haircuts by threatening to retaliate in some way through its regulatory power."

Nonsense, argued Eliot Spitzer, who as New York attorney general was way ahead of the curve in challenging Wall

Street arrogance. Writing in *Slate* on November 23, 2009, Spitzer pointed out: "Pressuring Goldman and the other counterparties to offer concessions would have forced them to absorb the consequences of making suspect deals with an insurance company that was essentially a Ponzi scheme."

The Ponzi scheme brings us back full circle to the Clinton bubble. As the inspector general's report stated: "In 2000, the [Clinton administration–backed] Commodity Futures Modernization Act (CFMA) . . . barred the regulation of credit default swaps and other derivatives." Why did the financial geniuses of the Clinton administration seek to prevent that obviously needed regulation? Because the Clintonistas believed that the Wall Street guys knew what they were doing and that what was good for them was good for us lesser folk.

Sounds nonsensical today. The inspector general's report notes that AIG, because of the deregulatory law that Summers and Geithner pushed through, was "able to sell swaps on $72 billion worth of CDOs to counterparties without holding reserves that a regulated insurance company would be required to maintain." But why, then, was Summers once again running the show with Geithner, when both have made careers of exhibiting total contempt for the public interest? Because there is no accountability for the high rollers of finance, no matter who happens to be president.

Defenders of the Obama administration justified the appointment of the likes of Summers and Geithner as necessary in order to enlist their expertise in unraveling the market disaster they had helped create. And on June 15, 2009, five months after Obama's inauguration, in a column they jointly wrote for the *Washington Post*, the pair at last publicly confronted the error of their ways. Not directly, of course, for accountability is hardly the mark of either man. "Over the past two years, we have faced the most severe financial crisis since the Great Depression," they wrote, placing the blame squarely where it belongs, on the unregulated derivatives markets they once gushed over. "This current financial crisis had many causes . . . in the widespread use of poorly understood financial instruments, in shortsightedness and excessive leverage at financial institutions. But it was also the product of basic failures in financial supervision and regulation."

What irony that Summers, who as Clinton's Treasury secretary pushed through legislation guaranteeing "Legal Certainty for Swap Agreements" and banning the regulation of securitized mortgage debt, should now admit that "securitization led to an erosion of lending standards, resulting in market failure that fed the housing boom and deepened the housing bust."

According to Summers and Geithner, the Obama plan promised that all derivatives dealers would be "subject to supervision, and regulators will be empowered to enforce rules against manipulation and abuse." If such language is ever passed into law, I hope that Brooksley Born is in the gallery and gets the standing ovation she deserves as the woman who, as head of the Commodity Futures Trading Commission, warned that the derivatives market needed to be regulated. Summers and his predecessor Robert Rubin destroyed

Born's career because she dared to accurately predict today's crisis.

Better late than never. But there was no guarantee that the Obama plan, limited as it was, would not be subverted by the financial industry lobbyists, whose enormous campaign treasure chest, now financed by taxpayers, allows them to slice and dice congressional voting blocs the way they did subprime mortgages.

After squandering his first year in office catering to Wall Street, Obama suddenly attempted to shift course. It took a rebellion by Massachusetts voters in January 2010 to get him to pay full attention to the failures of his economic program. In the bluest of blue states, the voters who had given Obama a 26 percent plurality in the presidential election the year before spurned his personal entreaty to send another Democrat to fill the seat left vacant by the death of Senator Ted Kennedy. The message was understood by Obama, who the very next day fundamentally altered his administration's response to the economic meltdown. Or so it seemed for the moment.

The day after the Massachusetts rejection, the president returned to the views he had expressed in that Cooper Union speech during the Democratic primary and was once again a proponent of what he called the "spirit of Glass-Steagall." He suddenly endorsed former Fed chair Paul Volcker's proposal to restore the division between commercial and investment banking and threatened the banks with a tax on their profits to help defray the cost of the debacle. But the response of the Wall Street crowd to even those tepid calls for reform was swift and decisive in its impact.

"Buyer's remorse" is the way Senator John Cornyn, the Senate Republicans' fundraiser, gleefully referred to Wall Street moguls' current disenchantment with the U.S. president they thought they had bought. They didn't like it when Barack Obama, after a year of throwing trillions of American taxpayer dollars into the bailout sinkhole, dared remark that he had hoped there might be some return for ordinary folks trying to save their jobs and homes. Not just huge bonuses for the folks the president dared refer to as "fat cats."

That's it! the moguls declared, and promptly shifted their political donations from Democrats to Republicans. Among the unglued was James L. (Jamie) Dimon, a friend of Obama's from Chicago and darling of the Democratic Party, which enjoyed his generous donations. The *Times* reported that JPMorgan CEO Dimon received a $17-million bonus for his work in the year after his bank was bailed out on the taxpayer's dime. As the *Times*' David D. Kirkpatrick observed: "If the Democratic Party has a stronghold on Wall Street it is JPMorgan Chase . . . But this year Chase's political action committee is sending the Democrats a pointed message . . . It has rebuffed solicitations from the national Democratic House and Senate campaign committees. Instead it gave $30,000 to their Republican counterparts." Chump change, given the hundreds of millions that Wall Street doles out to buy legislation, but a warning shot nonetheless.

Dimon had lunch with the president to say he doesn't like this talk of forcing banks like Chase to decide whether they are working for federal insured depositors or are high rollers in the Wall Street investment casino. Joining Dimon and the president was Robert Wolf, chief of the U.S. division of the Swiss-owned bank UBS. Wolf, who played golf and watched fireworks with the president, was appointed by Obama to the Presidential Economic Recovery Advisory Board, headed by Volcker. Wolf was upset when Obama recently endorsed Volcker's proposal for restoring the spirit of the Glass-Steagall Act by separating investment from commercial banking.

They needn't have been overly worried. There wasn't much possibility of restoring Glass-Steagall after Obama wasted his filibuster-proof majority in the Senate by flummoxing heath care while ignoring banking reform. He had no more money to throw at the banks, so why should their lobbyists cooperate on financial reform legislation any more than the health insurance companies did on their issues?

All he had left were verbal arrows, and surely $145 billion in banking bonuses for devastating the U.S. economy supports Obama's all-too-rare rhetorical jabs at a rapacious Wall Street. How else to counter Sarah Palin and the Tea Party members who blasted the big government bailouts as if they represent an Obama invention rather than a creation of the last Republican White House? Since Bill Clinton's presidency, the only difference in the two parties' programs was over who best served Wall Street and hence deserved to be more handsomely rewarded with campaign funding.

Take the mask off the Obama candidacy, and there was always a deeply disturbing reality that his massive Internet-driven grassroots contributor base concealed: Obama was the first major-party presidential candidate since Richard Nixon to base his campaign fundraising exclusively on private rather than public funds. But the appearance of all those coins flowing in from the common folk denied the harsh reality that his campaign contributions established him as the darling of Wall Street financiers—the very folks whose interests he served so faithfully during his first year in office as he endorsed, and indeed expanded, the Bush bailout.

While his base was distracted with a never very bold health care proposal, designed to mollify the insurance companies while providing at least the appearance of universal health care, Obama ceded the genuinely populist cause in the midst of a banking meltdown by coddling Wall Street. It was only a year into his administration, at a point when the banks had obviously failed to deliver on a promise to aid distressed homeowners and increase lending, that Obama in direct response to adverse poll results once again sounded the populist notes of the early months of his primary campaign.

And for that too-little-too-late response to the catastrophic economic crisis they caused, Wall Street titans now took Obama to the woodshed to teach him and the Democrats a lesson about who's really in control.

Obama got the message and caved. It would be the defining moment of his presidency, as he subsequently backtracked on even his very modest demands for financial reform that so alarmed Wall Street. By being unwilling to confront Wall Street, he surrendered the substance as well as the rhetoric of a meaningful populist response to the faux insurgents of the Tea Party and Sarah Palin, who had become their head yell leader. Suddenly the bailout was the responsibility not of George W. Bush, who initiated it, but rather Obama, who inherited it. What an odd moment to witness a Democrat elected on a promise of change paying homage to the lions of the financial establishment at a moment when they least deserved it.

Shortly after he was attacked by Dimon and Blankfein for daring to criticize the banking moguls, Obama in an interview with *Business Week* and Bloomberg suddenly reversed course. "I know both those guys, and they are very savvy businessmen," he said. "I, like most of the American people, don't begrudge people success or wealth . . . That is part of the free market system." He then went on to compare their success that had little to do with a "free-market" system with that of star baseball players who are indeed rewarded by their success in giving free-market consumers what they want. The two businessmen in question did quite the opposite, using marketing to deceive their customers.

None more so than African Americans, the vast majority of whom had voted for Obama but who were the group hardest hit in the mortgage meltdown, which both Dimon's JPMorgan Chase and Blankfein's Goldman Sachs had done so much to create and profit from. As Blankfein is well aware: his 2007 bonus was an industry record–breaking $68.7 million, a third of it in cash, according to the *Washington Post*, while his company, Goldman Sachs, made $11 billion. In 2009, after its bailout, Goldman made a record profit of $13.4 billion. That year, amid an atmosphere of public anger over bonuses, Blankfein took a $9-million bonus.

Obama may know "those guys" who created this mess, and they certainly contributed massively to his campaign, but does he keep in touch with the community folks back in Chicago whom he once enlisted to organize and who were now suffering as much as any in the nation? As one report by the CBS affiliate in Chicago on December 15, 2009, headlined: "Foreclosures Plague African American Neighborhoods." But that was the norm throughout the country, where black and Hispanic communities had been the most exposed to dubious mortgage offerings. Again quoting the local CBS report: "So why is this hitting African American neighborhoods so hard? CBS 2 is told it started with loans that had bad terms being pushed in that community more."

A *New York Times* survey of lending practices in New York City "found that black households making more than $68,000 a year were nearly five times as likely to hold high interest subprime mortgages as whites of similar or even lower incomes." The pattern has been well documented throughout the nation, but that did not galvanize an administration headed by the first African American president to do much to stop the foreclosure avalanche. An Obama program that paid out $75 billion to banks to help prevent home mortgage foreclosures had by January 2010, ten months after its inception, produced only 31,000 mortgage adjustments on one million applications. JPMorgan Chase, which had acquired Washington Mutual, a major subprime mortgage lender, while receiving $25 billion in bailout funds, was one of the worst offenders in forcing people from their homes.

The bailout money was used to make the banks whole, and indeed the two bankers defended by Obama had paid back their loans, but not the far greater costs of the low-interest backing they received from the government and of the enormous cost of the government purchasing toxic derivatives that the banks had led the way in packaging. Nor was there any payback for the far larger damage to the entire world's economies, including our nation's. In the end, nothing very significant would be undertaken by the Obama administration to mitigate the pain of this crash or to avoid a subsequent one, for it would involve fundamentally challenging the prerogatives of power enjoyed by the very people who created the crisis in the first place.

This story ends as it began, with the greedy bankers and the politicians who loved them. And among those politicians of varied party and background were a movie-actor-turned-president, a patrician father and son team who each occupied the White House, an Arkansas poor boy who catered to the rich as if he were one of them, and the first nonwhite president who sadly enough proved to be not all that different in terms of whose interests he served.

In the end, Obama dropped the ball. The financial reform package his administration pushed through a Democratic-controlled Congress in the summer of 2010 provided precious little in the way of structural change in the markets. Although the economy was still floundering and Noble Prize–winning economist Paul Krugman was predicting a decade of stagnation possibly amounting to another Great Depression, with tens of millions of our citizens suffering, the president ignored their pain. Obama's economic team once again catered to Wall Street's demands that its financiers continue to be legally free to plunder. It was the final nail in the coffin of the New Deal, burying the dream that representative democracy could hold the multinational corporations accountable.

The dispiriting lesson of both the Clinton and the Obama White Houses is that the Democrats proved to be as eager to please Wall Street as their Republican rivals. The influence of big corporate money far overwhelms that of labor, environmental, consumer, or grassroots organizations, making a mockery of the American ideal of self-government when it comes to reining in the antics of the largest conglomerates of wealth.

It is a depressing message on which to conclude a book, I know, but hopefully an aroused public tired of getting ripped off by the apologists will someday act to force change and prove my gloomy prognosis wrong. Otherwise, we are destined for even greater trouble.

ACKNOWLEDGMENTS

I dedicated this book to Narda Zacchino not at all because she is my wife but rather because as my editor she has held me to the same high journalistic standards she adhered to during her three decades at the *Los Angeles Times*, where she rose to become the associate editor and a vice president. Working at the *Times* during her tenure there in much less exalted positions I witnessed up-close her courageous battles to hold high the banners of honesty, compassion, and fairness both at the paper and in her outside work at the American Society of Newspaper Editors and as a four-time Pulitzer Prize judge.

The superb Narda also deserves much credit for inspiring Peter Scheer, to whom this book is also dedicated, to become the excellent managing editor of Truthdig. Peter ran the editorial side of the magazine, with considerable input from our very skilled associate editor Kasia Anderson, allowing us to win a third prestigious Webby award as the Internet's "best political blog" during the time I was more focused on writing this book. But it was Truthdig that provided me with a vital forum for testing—some would say venting—my ideas on the banking meltdown, and I am grateful for the support of all there.

There would be no Truthdig were it not for our publisher, Zuade Kaufman, who first worked with me on my local columns for the *Los Angeles Times*, where, thanks to her efforts, we broke some important stories. She deserves a great deal of the credit for the conception and trajectory of Truthdig as a worthy model for Internet journalism. At USC Annenberg School for Communication and Journalism, where Zuade received her master's degree in journalism inspired much by the legendary Ed Guthman, the wall between the demands of the business side and the obligations of a journalistic enterprise were taken very seriously, and witnessing Zuade maintain that wall in a harsh financial climate when other news outlets are compromising has been nothing short of inspiring. Truthdig has thrived under her principled leadership, aided by four other Annenberg scholars: John Cheney, Kassandra Zuanich, and the aforementioned Peter and Kasia. The extremely capable executive assistant Lucy Berbeo was educated elsewhere, but her cool competence has been vital to our enterprise.

The Annenberg School has not only been an incubator for Truthdig but also has provided me with a paying job as a professor and the opportunity to engage hundreds of generally wonderful students whose intelligence, curiosity, and idealism helped me overcome the cynical dismissal by some of my peers of this generation as one who neither reads nor cares about important issues. I have many wonderful colleagues at Annenberg, but space permits thanking only Geoff Cowan, who as dean had the courage to hire me when I was under considerable attack from local right-wing media pundits for my columns in the *Los Angeles Times,* and my Communication Department chair Larry Gross, who is both smarter and more controversial in his thoughts than I am and yet manages to succeed splendidly in the academic world without selling out.

My other two sons, Christopher and Joshua, were more directly connected with this book, as indicated on the title page. This is my second book in which Josh has done the heavy lifting on research and I believe that even as a parent I am being objective in praising his enormous talent as a researcher, which provided ample ammunition to shred the tissue of lies that powerful corporations and politicians use to conceal their chicanery. Christopher, who collaborated with me in our writing work for Oliver Stone's film *Nixon,* was the primary author of the book we did on the Iraq War. That he is an extraordinary writer is reflected in many of this book's more polished passages.

My agent, Steve Wasserman, and Carl Bromley, editor of Nation Books, guided this project from its inception, and Carl proved much deserving of his considerable reputation as a super-sharp and broadly informed editor. His ever-deft humor made the heeded criticisms palatable. Tom Caswell, the brilliant copyeditor of Truthdig, along with meticulous proofreader Barbra Frank, did much to make the manuscript comprehensible, as did Perseus project editor Sandra Beris and copyeditor Beth Wright. Needless to say, any errors that slipped through are mine alone.

NOTES

1. IT *WAS* THE ECONOMY, STUPID

1 **"How did this happen?":** Henry Paulson Jr., *On the Brink. Inside the Race to Stop the Collapse of the Global Financial System* (New York: Hachette, 2010), 861–867, Kindle2 2.

1 **"It was a humbling question":** Ibid.

2 **"perfect storm":** Evan Thomas and Michael Hirsch, "Rubin's Detail Deficit," *Newsweek*, December 8, 2008.

11 **"irrational exuberance":** Alan Greenspan, remarks at the Annual Dinner and Francis Boyer Lecture of the American Enterprise Institute for Public Policy Research, Washington, DC, December 5, 1996, www.federalreserve.gov/boardDocs/speeches/1996/19961205.htm.

16 **"I don't think the worst is over":** Chrystia Freeland, "Lunch with the FT: Larry Summers," *Financial Times*, July 10, 2009, www.ft.com/cms/s/2/6ac06592–6ce0 –11de-af56–00144feabdc0.html.

16 **"In a recession this deep":** Robert Reich, Robert Reich's Blog, July 2009, robertreich.blogspot.com/2009/07/when-will-recovery-begin-never.html.

16 **"Until consumers start spending again":** Ibid.

18   **"The American experiment has worked in large part because":** Remarks of Senator Barack Obama, "Renewing the American Economy," Cooper Union, New York, March 27, 2008.

20   *Fortune* **magazine was headlined "Robert Rubin":** Katie Benner, "Robert Rubin: What Meltdown?" CNNMoney.com, January 31, 2008, money.cnn.com/2008/01/31/news/economy/rubin_benner.fortune/index.htm?postversion=2008013113.

21   **"A lending catastrophe":** Ibid.

22   **"This loss has not happened by accident":** Obama, "Renewing the American Economy."

23   **"Unfortunately, instead of establishing a 21st century":** Ibid.

24   **"the $300 million lobbying":** Ibid.

2. THE HIGH PRIESTESS OF THE REAGAN REVOLUTION

26   **"called her 'The Margaret Thatcher of financial regulation'":** Wendy Gramm, Mercatus Center Distinguished Senior Scholar, Mercatus Center, George Mason University, mercatus.org/wendy-gramm.

27   **"Unfortunately, this legislation does not deal":** Ronald Reagan, Remarks on Signing the Garn–St. Germain Depository Institutions Act of 1982, October 15, 1982, www.reagan.utexas.edu/archives/speeches/1982/101582b.htm.

28   **"Ronald Reagan's dream of carrying out a sweeping":** Richard Hornik, "Shortening the Tether on Bankers," *Time*, August 17, 1987.

29   **"the 1933 Glass-Steagall Act restrictions on securities activities":** Ronald Reagan, Statement on Signing Competitive Equality Banking Act of 1987, August 10, 1987, www.presidency.ucsb.edu/ws/index.php?pid=34677.

30   **"These new anti-consumer and anti-competitive pro-
     visions could hold back a vital service industry"**: Ibid.

30   **"Oh, yuck"**: Richard L. Berke, "Tough Texan: Phil
     Gramm," *New York Times*, February 19, 1995.

31   **"in 1981, I wrote the first"**: "Senator Phil Gramm An-
     nounces His Retirement," CNN transcript, September
     4, 2001, transcripts.cnn.com/Transcripts/0109/04/bn
     .11.html.

35   **"Soothing Words About Derivatives"**: "Soothing
     Words About Derivatives: Futures Regulator Says Risks
     Have Been Exaggerated," *American Banker*, September
     21, 1992.

36   **"Lately, I've been hearing various regulators"**: Ibid.

36   **"First, there is [the] notion"**: Ibid.

37   **"The Monster That Ate Wall Street"**: Matthew
     Philips, "The Monster That Ate Wall Street: How
     'credit default swaps'—an insurance against bad loans—
     turned from a smart bet into a killer," *Newsweek*, Octo-
     ber 6, 2008.

38   **"As to the concern that derivatives are too esoteric"**:
     "Soothing Words."

38   **"Finally, the idea that derivatives"**: Ibid.

41   **"Much has been said about the growth"**: Dr. Wendy
     L. Gramm, Statement on Financial Derivatives Supervi-
     sory Improvement Act of 1998 Before the Committee
     on Banking and Financial Services, U.S. House of Rep-
     resentatives, July 17, 1998, financialservices.house.gov/
     banking/71798gra.htm.

45   **"GE Capital flourished as a member"**: "What's Wrong
     with General Electric," *Economist*, March 19, 2009.

3. THE CLINTON BUBBLE

51   **"Common practices uncovered by the investigation"**:
     Jill M. Hendrickson, "The Long and Bumpy Road to

Glass-Steagall Reform: A Historical and Evolutionary Analysis of Banking Legislation," *American Journal of Economics and Sociology* 60, no. 4 (2001): 849–879.

52 **"They have announced a $70 billion merger":** Editorial, "A Monster Merger," *New York Times*, April 8, 1998.

53 **"In a single day, with a single bold merger, pending":** Leslie Wayne, "Shaping a Colossus: The Politics; Deal Jump-Starts a Stalled Banking Bill," *New York Times*, April 8, 1998.

54 **"Indeed, within 24 hours of the deal's":** Ibid.

55 **"Over the [past] seven years, we have tried":** Statement by President Bill Clinton at the Signing of the Financial Modernization Bill, Office of Public Affairs, U.S. Department of the Treasury, November 12, 1999, www.ustreas.gov/press/releases/ls241.htm.

56 **"In the 1930s, at the trough of the Depression":** Ibid.

57 **"a nation of whiners":** Patrice Hill, "McCain Adviser Talks of 'Mental Recession,'" *Washington Times*, July 9, 2008.

57 **"I think we will look back in ten":** David Leonhardt, "Washington's Invisible Hand," *New York Times*, September 26, 2008.

57 **"Citigroup threatens no one":** "A Monster Merger."

58 **"Sandy suddenly suggested, 'We should call Clinton'":** Monica Langley, *Tearing Down the Walls: How Sandy Weill Fought His Way to the Top of the Financial World . . . and Then Nearly Lost It All* (New York: Simon & Schuster, 2003), 5593–5598, Kindle2 2.

60 **"I would compartmentalize the industry":** Bob Ivry, "Reed Says 'I'm Sorry' for Role in Creating Citigroup," Bloomberg, November 6, 2009, www.bloomberg.com/apps/news?pid=20601109&sid=albMYVE7D578.

60 **"No private enterprise should be allowed":** William Safire, "Essay: Don't Bank on It," *New York Times*, April 16, 1998.

63 **"I developed a particularly good relationship":** Sandy Weill and Judah S. Kraushaar, *The Real Deal: My Life in Business and Philanthropy* (New York: Hachette, 2006), 6132–6137, Kindle2 2.

64 **"By early 1999, prospects":** Ibid., 6143–6148.

65 **"indicated a far more flexible stance":** Ibid, 6146–6151.

65 **"his most important trump card":** Langley, *Tearing Down Walls*, 6694–6699.

66 **"the Congressional Black Caucus expressed":** Weill, *The Real Deal*, 6152–6157.

66 **"I had met Jesse several years before":** Ibid., 6153–6157.

67 **"The impasse threatened":** Langley, *Tearing Down Walls*, 6691–6696.

68 **"The civil rights leader developed":** Ibid., 99–104.

68 **"Just as we were about to cross the goal line":** Weill, *The Real Deal*, 6158–6163.

69 **"I thought the worst":** Ibid.

69 **Now Jackson came to the defense:** Langley, *Tearing Down Walls*, 6699–6704.

70 **"The final hurdle to passage of the bill was":** Editorial, "Breaking Glass-Steagall," *Nation*, November 15, 1999.

72 **"President Clinton soon signed into law":** Langley, *Tearing Down Walls*, 6710–6716.

72 **he and Phil Gramm joked:** Weill, *The Real Deal*, 6166–6171.

73 **"Adorning a conference room wall on the third floor":** Timothy L. O'Brien and Julie Creswell, "Laughing All the Way from the Bank," *New York Times*, September 11, 2005.

74 **"Glass-Steagall, the hoary law that Citigroup's":** Ibid.

75   **"The most important consequence of the repeal of Glass-Steagall":** Joseph E. Stiglitz, "Capitalist Fools," *Vanity Fair* (January 2009).

77   **"lending at high rates to low-income American borrowers":** "American Banking—Weill Business: Citigroup Buys Associates First Capital," *Economist*, September 9, 2000.

77   **"There are serious problems with Citigroup's failure":** Maude Hurd, "Citi-Associates Blessing Rewards Wrongdoing: Citigroup Inc. Buys Associates First Capital Corp.," *American Banker*, December 8, 2000.

77   **"The pattern of racially and economically bifurcated lending":** Ibid.

78   **"Citigroup's investment banking arm scooped":** Eric Dash, "Citigroup Buys Parts of a Troubled Mortgage Lender," *New York Times*, September 1, 2007.

     4. THE VALIANT STAND OF BROOKSLEY BORN

82   **"Committee to Save the World":** *Time* cover, February 15, 1999.

83   **"assures the economic utility of the futures markets":** U.S. Commodity Futures Trading Commission, Statement of Mission and Responsibilities, www.cftc.gov/About/MissionResponsibilities/index.htm.

84   **"I became concerned about it once I got to the commission":** "A Conversation with Brooksley Born," *Washington Lawyer* (October 2003), www.dcbar.org/for_lawyers/resources/legends_in_the_law/born.cfm.

84   **"[Born's] comments in speeches and in a discussion":** Michael Schroeder and Greg Ip, "Out of Reach: The Enron Debacle Spotlights Huge Void in Financial Regulation," *Wall Street Journal*, December 13, 2001.

84   **"regulatory staff and lawmakers":** Ibid.

85   "You are welcome to claim": Ibid.

85   "fanatical about preventing any hint": Ibid.

86   "Rubin, among others, says the joy of working with
      Greenspan": Joshua Cooper Ramo, "The Three Marke-
      teers," *Time*, February 15, 1999.

86   "The quiet romance of the man": Ibid.

86   "more like an investment bank": Ibid.

86   "intellect never fails to dazzle": Ibid.

87   "What holds them together is a passion for think-
      ing": Ibid.

89   "They believed that we all had a responsibility":
      Brooksley Born, interview with Narda Zacchino, Sep-
      tember 18, 2009.

89   "ferocious sense of injustice": "A Conversation with
      Brooksley Born."

91   "I had been representing foreign entities": Born, in-
      terview with Zacchino.

92   This allowed the business to expand: "A Conversation
      with Brooksley Born."

92   She noted that the CFTC: Ibid.

93   "was a nightmare waiting to happen": Ibid.

94   There were no hearings: Ibid.

94   "some members of this group thought that deriva-
      tives": Robert E. Rubin and Jacob Weisberg, *In an Uncer-
      tain World: Tough Choices from Wall Street to Washington*
      (New York: Random House, 2003), 4782–4787, Kindle2.

94   "Not anyone in that group indicated to me": Born,
      interview with Zacchino.

95   "I walk into Brooksley's office one day": Michael
      Greenberger, interview with *PBS Frontline*, July 14, 2009.

95   "according to people with knowledge": Schroeder
      and Ip, "Out of Reach."

95   "fanatical about preventing any hint of derivatives":
      Ibid.

96 "I thought it was very bad policy, but on the other hand": "A Conversation with Brooksley Born."

96 "blank check to operate": Schroeder and Ip, "Out of Reach."

97 "I always felt that the titans": Peter S. Goodman, "Taking Hard New Look at a Greenspan Legacy," *New York Times*, October 9, 2008.

98 "The sudden failure or abrupt withdrawal": Ibid.

98 "risks in financial markets, including derivatives markets": Ibid.

99 "'Well, Brooksley, I guess you and I will never agree'": Rick Schmitt, "Prophet and Loss," *Stanford Magazine* (April/March 2009).

100 "Clinton made a deal with Greenspan": Robert Reich, interview with the author, October 2009.

100 "The three men have a mania for analysis": Ramo, "The Three Marketeers."

101 "history already has shown that Greenspan was wrong": Schmitt, "Prophet and Loss."

101 "asked Congress to immediately pass legislation": Jerry Knight, "Agencies Try to Block Study on Derivatives," *Washington Post*, June 6, 1998.

102 "Born did not propose imposing regulations": Ibid.

102 "As you know, Mr. Chairman": Treasury Deputy Undersecretary Lawrence H. Summers, Testimony Before the Senate Committee on Agriculture, Nutrition and Forestry, July 30, 1998, www.ustreas.gov/press/releases/rr2616.htm.

103 "Mr. Chairman, the American OTC derivatives market": Ibid.

103 "First, the parties to these kinds of contracts": Ibid.

104 "The nation's top financial regulators wish": Michael Schroeder, "CFTC Chief Refuses to Take Back Seat in Derivatives Debate," *Wall Street Journal*, November 3, 1998.

105   **"huge exposure to derivatives threatened":** Ibid.

106   **it "would prevent the Commission from taking action":** CFTC Chair Brooksley Born, Testimony Before
the U.S. House of Representatives Committee on Banking and Financial Services, July 24, 1998, www.cftc.gov/
opa/speeches/opaborn-33.htm.

106   **"No provision of the Commodity Exchange Act":**
Commodity Futures Modernization Act, www.sec.gov/
about/laws/cfma.pdf.

107   **"All tragedies in life are preceded by warnings":**
Michael Hirsh, "The Great Clash of '09," *Newsweek*, December 24, 2008, www.newsweek.com/id/176830.

108   **"explicitly exempted OTC derivatives":** "Over-the-
Counter Derivatives Markets Act of 2009," www.financial
stability.gov/docs/regulatoryreform/titleVII.pdf.

108   **"As a result, the market for OTC derivatives":** Ibid.

108   **"the most severe financial crisis since the Great Depression":** Timothy Geithner and Lawrence Summers,
"A New Financial Foundation," *Washington Post*, June
15, 2009.

109   **"This current financial crisis":** Ibid.

5. THEY HAVE NO SHAME

115   **"Last year, as Congress and the Clinton administra-
tion":** Joseph Kahn and Jeff Gerth, "Enron's Collapse:
The Politics; Collapse May Reshape the Battlefield of
Deregulation," *New York Times*, December 4, 2001.

116   **"Here I am the only member of Congress":** Alan
Grayson, radio interview, www.rollcall.com/news/
39933-1.html.

116   **"Enron is the sequel to California":** Kahn and Gerth,
"Enron's Collapse."

116   **"Enron was getting very heavily into derivatives":** Ibid.

117   **"A year ago, when most of the political world":**
Michael Schroeder and Greg Ip, "Out of Reach: The

Enron Debacle Spotlights Huge Void In Financial Regulation," *Wall Street Journal*, December 13, 2001.

118 **"negotiate major aspects of the bill directly with regulators":** Ibid.

118 **"That's at least partly because Enron":** Ibid.

119 **"The fact is, Lay and Enron were working Washington":** Stephen J. Hedges, Jeff Zeleny, and Frank James, "Enron 'Players' Worked D.C. Ties," *Chicago Tribune*, January 13, 2002.

120 **"Enron made a $100,000 contribution in 1997":** Ibid.

120 **"with Kantor's help in Croatia":** Walter V. Robinson, "Donations Are Linked to Kantor Trade Missions," *Boston Globe*, February 12, 1997.

120 **"Enron officials were so often part":** Jack Douglas Jr and Jennifer Autrey, "How Enron Massaged the Political Process," *Fort Worth Star-Telegram*, January 27, 2002.

121 **"During his nine-month tenure at Commerce, Kantor":** Robinson, "Donations Are Linked to Kantor Trade Missions."

122 **"On November 22, 1995 . . . Clinton scrawled":** Michael Weisskopf, "The White House: That Invisible Mack Sure Can Leave His Mark," *Time*, September 1, 1997.

123 **"This is an extremely dynamic":** Judy Sarasohn, "Enron Hire Faces Some Partisan Fire," *Washington Post*, October 12, 2000.

123 **He cited, accurately, her "experience":** Ibid.

124 **"Treasury just minutes ago sent this compromise language":** Eric Lipton, "Gramm and the 'Enron Loophole,'" *New York Times*, November 14, 2008.

125 **Three days after that e-mail boasting of the progress:** Ibid.

126 **In a subsequent e-mail Long:** Ibid.

126 **"Before its collapse in 2001":** Mark Jickling, Specialist in Financial Economics Government and Finance Divi-

sion, "The Enron Loophole," Congressional Research
Service report, July 7, 2008, Order Code RS22912.

127 **"Because of Enron's new, unregulated":** Public Citizen,
*Blind Faith: How Deregulation and Enron's Influence Over
Government Looted Billions from Americans,* December 2001.

127 **thousands of hours of audiotapes:** Transcripts of
Enron trader conversations, obtained and released by
the Snohomish County Public Utility District, published
by *Seattle Times,* June 2, 2004, seattletimes
.nwsource.com/html/localnews/2001945474_web
enronaudio02.html.

128 **In one of the taped conversations:** Ibid.

129 **"Enron employees talked openly":** Snohomish
County Public Utility District, "Our Fight Against
Enron," Newsroom/Special Reports, www.snopud
.com/newsroom/SpecialReports/enron.ashx?p=1326.

131 **"appears to be very free market":** E-mail from Wendy
Gramm reprinted in Eric Lipton, "Gramm and the
'Enron Loophole,'" *New York Times,* November 14, 2008.

131 **"From: Wgramm@aol.com 02/14/2001":** Ibid.

133 **"an overseer of Enron's financial reporting, internal":** Public Citizen, *Blind Faith,* citing Enron's Schedule 14a filings from 1998 to 2001, www.sec.gov/edgar/
searchedgar/formpick.htm.

135 **"even some Republicans were saying":** John Nichols,
"Enron: What Dick Cheney Knew," *Nation,* March 28,
2002.

135 **"a man who had headed a corporation with extensive business":** Ibid.

136 **"called Treasury Undersecretary Peter Fisher":** Minority Staff Special Investigations Division, Committee
on Government Reform, U.S. House of Representatives, "Bush Administration Contacts with Enron," Prepared for Rep. Henry A. Waxman, May 2002.

136   **"I prefaced our conversation":** Robert E. Rubin and
       Jacob Weisberg, *In an Uncertain World: Tough Choices
       from Wall Street to Washington* (New York: Random
       House, 2003), 5638–5643, Kindle2.

137   **"Of course, in the wake of Enron's implosion":** Ibid.,
       5641–5645.

137   **"probably a bad idea":** Ibid., 5638–5643.

137   **"our extraordinarily effective congressional liaison":**
       Ibid., 4501–4506.

6. ROBERT RUBIN RAKES IT IN AT CITIGROUP

140   **he was Citi's "resident sage":** Eric Dash and Julie
       Creswell, "Citigroup Saw No Red Flags Even as It Made
       Bolder Bets," *New York Times*, November 22, 2008.

141   **"Working in the financial sector":** Robert E. Rubin
       and Jacob Weisberg, *In an Uncertain World: Tough Choices
       from Wall Street to Washington* (New York: Random
       House, 2003), 5039–5046, Kindle2.

141   **"a reasonably commercial person":** Ibid.

141   **"something that would be financially rewarding":** Ibid.

142   **"On derivatives, yeah":** *This Week* with former presi-
       dent Bill Clinton and Jake Tapper, ABC transcript, April
       18, 2010.

144   **"pooled $492 million worth of mortgages":** John
       Dunbar and David Donald, "The Roots of the Finan-
       cial Crisis: Who Is to Blame? Banks that Financed Sub-
       prime Industry Collecting Billions in Bailouts," The
       Center for Public Integrity, May 6, 2009, www.public
       integrity.org/investigations/economic_meltdown/
       articles/entry/1286.

144   **"Demonizing the bankers":** "New Citi Chair: Bankers
       Aren't Villains: Everybody 'Has Some Part of the
       Blame' for Financial Crisis, Richard Parsons Says," CBS
       / Associated Press, April 7, 2009.

145 **"it extends Citi's already huge credit-card opera-tion"**: "American Banking—Weill Business: Citigroup Buys Associates First Capital," *Economist*, September 9, 2000.

145 **"We're disappointed to see Citigroup"**: Pamela Yip, "Citigroup Closes $27 Billion Acquisition of Associates First Capital Corp.," *Dallas Morning News*, December 1, 2000.

145 **"Associates has a notable record"**: Maude Hurd, "Citi-Associates Blessing Rewards Wrongdoing (Citi-group Inc. Buys Associates First Capital Corp.)," *American Banker*, December 8, 2000.

147 **"He [Arnall] said: 'We've started to make some changes'"**: Brian C. Mooney, Patrick's Path from Courtroom to Boardroom," *Boston Globe*, August 13, 2006.

148 **in "a very short phone conversation" the governor vouched:** Frank Phillips, "Governor Made Call on Be-half of Lender: Troubled Ameriquest Sought Infusion of Cash," *Boston Globe*, March 6, 2007.

148 **The *New York Times* later reported that the cash to-taled:** Eric Dash, "Citigroup Buys Parts of a Troubled Mortgage Lender," *New York Times*, September 1, 2007.

149 **"It is not going to be a subprime shop.":** Ibid.

149 **"Citigroup will also take over servicing rights":** Ibid.

150 **it "just missed doubling its CDO underwriting":** Asset Securitization Report, January 8, 2007.

151 **supposedly "learned for the first time":** Dash and Creswell, "Citigroup Saw No Red Flags."

151 **"Where Was the Wise Man?":** Nelson D. Schwartz and Eric Dash, "Where Was the Wise Man?" *New York Times*, April 27, 2008.

152 **"I've thought about that. I honestly don't know":** Ibid.

152 **"Modest and genial to a fault":** Ibid.

152 **"The bank's downfall was years in the making"**: Dash and Creswell, "Citigroup Saw No Red Flags."

153 **"And since joining Citigroup in 1999"**: Ibid.

154 **"Chuck was totally new to the job"**: Ibid.

155 **Citi "used accounting maneuvers to move billions"**: Ibid.

155 **"I just think senior managers got addicted"**: Ibid.

155 **a form called a "CDO liquidity put"**: Evan Thomas and Michael Hirsch, "Rubin's Detail Deficit," *Newsweek*, December 8, 2008.

156 **"Actually, I'm probably close to twenty years"**: Ibid.

158 **"doom a Dynegy merger"**: Rubin and Weisberg, *In an Uncertain World*, 5039–5046.

158 **"In that context, I placed a call to Peter Fisher"**: Ibid., 5635–5640.

159 **Citigroup was "a creditor of Enron"**: Ibid.

159 **"Many feared that the economy as a whole"**: Ibid., 5631–5636.

159 **"probably a bad idea"**: Ibid., 5635–5640.

159 **"an important public policy concern"**: Ibid.

159 **in fact the "parochial concern"**: Ibid.

160 **"If Rubin had succeeded in persuading Fisher"**: Mark R. Levin, "Covering Rubin: Senate Dems Work for the Ex-Treasury Secretary," January 3, 2003, *National Review Online*, article.nationalreview.com/267546/covering -rubin/mark-r-levin.

160 **"will probably be no more than a footnote"**: Mark Lewis, "Rubin Red-Faced Over Enron? Not in the *Times*," *Forbes*, February 11, 2002.

161 **"what he did was legal"**: "Four Committees in Search of a Scandal," *Economist*, January 17, 2002.

162 **It is "really hard to sue lawyers"**: Patrice Hill, "Enron Lawsuit Portrays Rubin as Pushing Bailout," *Washington Times*, April 9, 2002.

162   **"The banks named as defendants":** *The Regents of the University of California, et al., Plaintiffs, vs. Kenneth L. Lay, et al.*, www.universityofcalifornia.edu/news/enron/consolidated_complaint.pdf.

162   **bankers "swore" that they would "erect so-called Chinese Walls":** *Businessweek*, March 25, 2002, cited in ibid.

163   **Chinese walls are porous:** Ibid.

163   **"Between them, Citigroup and J.P. Morgan served as lead":** "Next Stop on Enron Express: Wall Street," Dow Jones News Service, February 26, 2002, cited in *Regents vs. Lay*.

164   **"In late 11/01, J.P. Morgan and Citigroup were desperately":** *Regents vs. Lay*, 356.

165   **"Citigroup's relationships with Enron":** Ibid., 357.

165   **"Citigroup actively engaged and participated in the fraudulent scheme":** Ibid.

166   **"In interacting with Enron, Citigroup functioned":** Ibid.

166   **"senior credit officers of Citigroup misrepresented":** Richard A. Oppel Jr. and Kurt Eichenwald, "Citigroup Said to Mold Deal to Help Enron Skirt Rules," *New York Times*, July 23, 2002.

166   **"Citigroup refused this week to answer repeated questions":** Daniel Altman, "How Citigroup Hedged Bets Against Enron," *New York Times*, February 8, 2002.

167   **"Everyone agrees we have to save Citi":** Thomas and Hirsch, "Rubin's Detail Deficit."

7. POVERTY PIMPS

171   **"Taxpayers are now on the hook":** Editorial, "Fannie Mae's Patron Saint," *Wall Street Journal*, September 9, 2008.

171   **"multibillion-dollar financial 'misstatement'":** Ibid.

174   **"Your letter also asked me about the impact":** Armando Falcon Jr., Testimony Before the Financial Crisis

Inquiry Commission, April 9, 2010,
fcic.gov/hearings/pdfs/2010-0409-Falcon.pdf.

176   **"one of the most powerful men in the United States"**:
Lloyd Grove, "The Big Chair: James Johnson, Head of
Brookings, Fannie Mae and the Kennedy Center, Is in
the Catbird Seat," *Washington Post*, March 27, 1998.

177   **A far less flattering portrait:** Matthew Cooper, "A
Medici with Your Money: Fannie Mae's Strategic Generosity," *Slate*, February 23, 1997.

178   **"other successful people who came into this Admin-
istration":** Richard W. Stevenson, "Man in the News:
Franklin Delano Raines; Moving from Big Money to
Politics," *New York Times*, April 13, 1996.

180   **"Countrywide's entire operation":** Gretchen Morgenson, "Inside the Countrywide Lending Spree," *New York
Times*, August 26, 2007.

181   **"to advise the corporation on issues":** "Fannie Mae
Names New Members to Its National Advisory Coun-
cil; Angelo R. Mozilo of Countrywide Credit Industries
Named Chairman," PR Newswire, March 6, 1996.

182   **"It was no secret in the industry that Freddie Mac officials":** Paul Muolo, "CFC Continues to Haunt Fannie
(Inside Take)," *National Mortgage News*, May 18, 2009.

182   **"Countrywide . . . the nation's largest independent":**
"Countrywide Announces Strategic Agreement with
Fannie Mae," PR Newswire, July 9, 1999.

183   **"The strategic agreement also addresses":** Ibid.

184   **"This new strategic agreement between Fannie Mae
and Countrywide":** Ibid.

184   **"Countrywide's monthly report underscored":** Hala
Habal, "Countrywide Beefing Up Subprime Mortgage
Loans," *American Banker*, October 7, 1999.

186   **"To have such an emotional connection to a home":**
Richard W. Stevenson, "A Homecoming at Fannie Mae:

Franklin Raines Takes Charge of a Most Political Company," *New York Times*, May 17, 1998.

188 **"We don't think that there is a housing bubble":** Aisha I. Jefferson, "Raines Bullish on Housing: Fannie Mae CEO Unconcerned About Potential Bubble," *Black Enterprise*, May 1, 2003.

188 **"Franklin D. Raines has a lot to smile about":** Ibid.

189 **"The point all of this makes, and the point we've been trying":** "Inside Fannie," *Wall Street Journal*, Review & Outlook, March 19, 2002.

189 **"to keep Fannie in the black":** Gretchen Morgenson, "They Left Fannie Mae, but We Got the Legal Bills," *New York Times*, September 5, 2009.

190 **"With all the turmoil of the financial crisis":** Ibid.

190 **"I cannot see the justification of people who led these organizations":** Ibid.

191 **"The *Wall Street Journal* finds problems":** Jefferson, "Raines Bullish on Housing."

192 **"Ultimately the companies were not unwitting victims":** Falcon, Testimony.

193 **"While all of this political power satisfied the egos":** Ibid.

8. GOLDMAN CLEANS UP

195 **"The first sound they'll hear":** Henry Paulson Jr., *On the Brink: Inside the Race to Stop the Collapse of the Global Financial System* (New York: Hachette, 2010), 199–204, Kindle2 2.

197 **"Like him, I am a firm believer in free markets":** Ibid., 221–226.

198 **in "recent history, there is a disturbance in the capital markets":** Ibid., 865–861.

198 **"I was convinced we were due":** Ibid., 858–864.

199 **"How did this happen?":** Ibid.

199   **"It was evident that the administration"**: Ibid., 864–870.

200   **"the lack of transparency of these CDS"**: Ibid., 879–885.

200   **"I misread the cause, and the scale"**: Ibid., 884–889.

201   **"It is a widely held view within the bank"**: Julie Creswell and Ben White, "The Guys from 'Government Sachs,'" *New York Times*, October 19, 2008.

204   **"Tim Geithner, president of the Federal Reserve Bank"**: Paulson, *On the Brink*, 877–882.

205   **"I don't see [it] imposing a serious problem."**: "Subprime Woes Likely Contained: Treasury's Paulson," Reuters, April 20, 2007.

205   **"I can't think of any situation where the backdrop"**: Les Christie, "Paulson: Subprime Help Needed—but No Bailout: Treasury Department Is Walking a Tightrope on Help for Mortgage Borrowers," CNNMoney.com, October 16, 2007, money.cnn.com/2007/10/16/real _estate/Paulson_leaning_on_lenders/index.htm.

205   **"The worst is likely to be behind us."**: "Paulson Says Worst of Financial Crisis Is Over," *Forbes*, May 7, 2008.

205   **"Basically they gave Congress a ransom note"**: Kathy Kiely and Sue Kirchhoff, "Leaders Back Historic Bailout: 'Now We Have to Get the Votes,'" *USA Today*, September 29, 2008.

206   **"I believe the most important part"**: Paulson, *On the Brink*, 175.

207   **"a leading architect of those bailouts"**: Jo Becker and Gretchen Morgenson, "Geithner, Member and Overseer of Finance Club," *New York Times*, April 27, 2009.

207   **"An examination of Mr. Geithner's five years"**: Ibid.

208   **"The New York Fed is, by custom and design, clubby and opaque."**: Ibid.

209   **"Hank, the American people don't like bailouts."**: Paulson, *On the Brink*, 3565–3571.

209   **"'How did we get to this point?' the president asked"**: Ibid., 199–204.

210 **"I explained that AIG differed from Lehman":** Ibid., 3706–3712.

213 **"The president found it hard to believe that an insurance company":** Ibid., 3713–3723.

213 **"Someday you guys are going to have to tell me":** Ibid., 3723–3728.

9. SUCKING UP TO THE BANKERS: CRISIS HANDOFF FROM BUSH TO OBAMA

217 **"But Wal-Mart, like other retailers":** Jason Furman, "Wal-Mart: A Progressive Success Story," *Center for American Progress*, November 28, 2005.

219 **"He had a baby face,":** Jo Becker and Gretchen Morgenson, "Geithner, Member and Overseer of Finance Club," *New York Times*, April 26, 2009.

219 **"Rubin, an old colleague from Goldman Sachs, told Paulson":** David Cho and Neil Irwin, "Familiar Trio at Heart of Citi Bailout: Rubin, Paulson, Geithner's Shared History Paved Way for $300 Billion Federal Guarantee," *Washington Post*, November 25, 2008.

220 **"The ultimate irony is":** Steven Pearlstein, "A Bailout Steeped in Irony," *Washington Post*, November 25, 2008.

220 **"a challenge more complex than any our financial system":** "Secretary Geithner Introduces Financial Stability Plan," U.S. Department of the Treasury, February 10, 2009, www.ustreas.gov/press/releases/tg18.htm.

221 **"Congress acted quickly and courageously":** Ibid.

221 **"the plan largely repeats the Bush administration's":** Stephen Labaton and Edmund L. Andrews, "Geithner Said to Have Prevailed on the Bailout," *New York Times*, February 10, 2009.

224 **"While Mr. Gensler is clearly an intelligent":** Ken Silverstein, "Senator Sanders Blocking Key Obama Nomination," *Harper's*, March 23, 2009.

225   **"OTC derivatives directly and indirectly support":**
       Treasury Undersecretary for Domestic Finance Gary
       Gensler, Testimony Before the House Committee on
       Risk Management, Research, and Specialty Crops, U.S.
       House of Representatives, May 18, 1999.

225   **"a powerful symbol of the kind of innovation":**
       Lawrence Summers, Testimony Before the Joint Senate
       Committees on Agriculture, Nutrition, and Forestry
       and Banking, Housing and Urban Affairs, June 21, 2000,
       www.ustreas.gov/press/releases/ls722.htm.

227   **"During the bubble, Goldman Sachs and other":** Edi-
       torial, "Betting Against All of Us," *New York Times*, De-
       cember 28, 2009.

229   **he deserved every penny of the nearly $8 million:**
       Philip Rucker, "Summers Raked in Speaking Fees from
       Wall Street," *Washington Post*, April 5, 2009.

230   **D.E. Shaw, a leading hedge fund:** Ibid.

230   **on top of the $586,996 he was paid as a professor:**
       Ibid.

230   **lecture fees, which in 2008 averaged $67,500:** Ibid.

230   **Lehman had purchased a 20 percent stake in D. E.
       Shaw:** D. E. Shaw Group Press Release, March 13, 2007,
       www.deshaw.com/articles/20070313.pdf.

230   **it paid him $135,000 for one appearance:** Jeff Zeleny,
       "Financial Industry Paid Millions to Obama Aide," *New
       York Times*, April 4, 2009.

231   **decided to turn over the $45,000 to a charity:** John D.
       McKinnon and T. W. Farnam, "Hedge Fund Paid Sum-
       mers $5.2 Million in Past Year," *Wall Street Journal*, April
       5, 2009.

231   **"widely recognized as one of the country's most dis-
       tinguished":** Zeleny, "Financial Industry."

231   **"has been at the forefront of this administration's
       work":** McKinnon and Farnam, "Hedge Fund."

232 **"First, the parties to these kinds of contracts":**
Deputy Treasury Secretary Lawrence H. Summers, Testimony Before the Senate Committee on Agriculture, Nutrition and Forestry, July 30, 1998.

232 **the plan carries "significant fraud risks,":** Office of the Special Inspector General for the Troubled Asset Relief Program (OSIGTARP), Quarterly Report to Congress, April 21, 2009.

233 **"Arguably, the wholesale failure of the credit rating":** Ibid.

233 **"The significant government-financed leverage":** Ibid.

234 **had made millions off his purchase:** Kate Kelly and Jon Hilsenrath, "New York Fed Chairman's Ties to Goldman Raise Questions," *Wall Street Journal*, May 4, 2009.

235 **"The Federal Reserve Bank of New York shaped":** Ibid.

236 **"Factors Affecting Efforts to Limit Payments":** OSIGTARP, "Factors Affecting Efforts to Limit Payments to AIG Counterparties," November 17, 2009.

236 **"Irrespective of their stated intent":** OSIGTARP, "Factors Affecting Efforts to Limit Payments."

236 **"The government could not unilaterally impose haircuts":** Herbert Allison, in a letter cited in "TARP Watchdog: N.Y. Fed 'Severely Limited' Savings on AIG," *PBS NewsHour*, November 17, 2009, www.pbs.org/newshour/updates/business/july-dec09/aig_11–17.html.

237 **"Pressuring Goldman and the other counterparties to offer concessions":** Eliot Spitzer, "Geithner's Disgrace: The New AIG Report Reveals How the Treasury Secretary—and U.S. Taxpayers—Were Fleeced by Wall Street Banks," *Slate*, November 23, 2009.

237 **"In 2000, the [Clinton administration–backed]":** OSIGTARP, "Factors Affecting Efforts to Limit Payments."

237 **"able to sell swaps on $72 billion":** Ibid.

238   **"Over the past two years, we have faced":** Timothy
       Geithner and Lawrence Summers, "A New Financial
       Foundation," *Washington Post*, June 15, 2009.

238   **"securitization led to an erosion of lending stan-
       dards":** Ibid.

238   **"subject to supervision, and regulators will be em-
       powered":** Ibid.

240   **"Buyer's remorse":** David D. Kirkpatrick, "In a Mes-
       sage to Democrats, Wall St. Sends Cash to G.O.P.," *New
       York Times*, February 8, 2010.

240   **"If the Democratic Party has a stronghold":** Ibid.

243   **"I know both those guys, and they are very savvy":**
       Julianna Goldman and Ian Katz, "Obama Doesn't 'Be-
       grudge' Bonuses for Blankfein, Dimon," *Business Week*,
       February 10, 2010.

244   **"Foreclosures Plague African American Neighbor-
       hoods.":** Pamela James, "Foreclosures Plague African
       American Neighborhoods," CBS 2 Chicago, December
       15, 2009, cbs2chicago.com/topstories/foreclosure
       .african.americans.2.1372346.html.

244   **A *New York Times* survey of lending practices:**
       Michael Powell, "Bank Accused of Pushing Mortgage
       Deals on Blacks," *New York Times*, June 7, 2009.

INDEX

ACC Capital Holdings, 78,
    146–147, 148–149
ACORN, 77, 145
African Americans
    and Fannie Mae disaster,
        178–179
    as hardest hit group in
        mortgage crisis, 244–245
    and Wall Street Project, 67
AIG (American International
        Group Inc.)
    backdoor bailout pays off
        banks at full value, 204,
        236–237
    bailout benefits Goldman,
        211, 223, 227
    compared to failed Lehman,
        210–212, 223
    Congress tracks bailout
        money, 228
    continuing failures rewarded
        with expanded rescues,
        222–223
    Paulson's bailout request to
        G. W. Bush, 210–213

Allstate Insurance, 203
Alt-A mortgages, 149, 174, 191
Alternative Servicing
        Compensation mortgage-
        backed securities (ASC
        MBS), 184
American Bar Association, 90
American Dream Initiative
        program, 178, 188
Ameriquest Mortgage, 146–149
Argent Mortgage, 78, 146–149
Arnall, Roland, 147–149
Arthur Andersen LLP, 117, 165,
        198
Associates First Capital, 76–77,
        144–145
Association of Community
        Organizations for
        Reform Now. See
        ACORN
Autrey, Jennifer, 120–121
Axelrod, David, 221

Backdoor bailout scheme,
        236–237

Bailouts
    Bowsher's warning, 98
    of Citigroup, 152–154,
        218–220
    of Fannie Mae Freddie Mac,
        GSEs, as private, profit-
        driven, 170–171, 189–190,
        197
    initiated by G. W. Bush,
        inherited by Obama, 170,
        210–213, 242–243
    of JPMorgan Chase, acquiring
        Washington Mutual, 245
    of Long-Term Capital
        Management, 84
    No Banker Left Behind
        program, 228
    paybacks lacking, 245
    Safire on, 60–61
    secret meetings of Paulson,
        Bernanke, Geithner,
        Blankfein, 206, 223
    take-it-or-leave-it proposal
        by Paulson to Congress,
        205–206
    See also AIG; Citigroup;
        Goldman Sachs
Bair, Sheila, 13
Baker, Dean, 167
Baker, James, III, 119
Bank of America, 181, 183
Banks, commercial
    consequences of
        deregulation, 75
    prevented from gambling by
        Glass-Steagall, 50–51, 60,
        241

Barofsky, Neil M., 232, 236
Bearings Bank, 93
Becker, Jo, 207–208, 219
Benner, Katie, 21
Bernanke, Ben
    in G. W. Bush–AIG bailout
        discussion, 213
    hires Enron lobbyist to
        protect Federal Reserve,
        115–116, 133
Blankfein, Lloyd, 223, 244
Bliley, Thomas, 65
Bloomberg, 243
Bolton, Joshua B., 201
Bonuses given to executives
    of AIG investigated by
        Congress, 228
    enlarge with Citigroup's
        CDO business, 155
    of Fannie Mae based on false
        figures, 187, 190, 192
    by Goldman to Blankfein,
        244
    by JPMorgan to Dimon, 240
    with no-strings-attached
        bailouts, 205
Born, Brooksley
    background, experience,
        88–92
    as CFTC chair, 37, 82–85
    derivatives study prohibited
        by Congress, 94, 101–104
    opposed by Rubin, 94,
        100–105
    opposed by Greenspan 82
    opposed by Summers, 95,
        102–103, 231

pressured by White House,
Treasury, Enron, 93–97
tries to regulate OTC
derivatives, futures
markets, 39, 41, 82–88,
92–93, 224
Bowsher, Charles A., 97–98
Brown, Ron, 121
Bubbles. *See* Financial bubbles
Buffett, Warren, 20, 82
Bundled derivatives, 9–10, 37–38
Bush, George H. W. (Bush I),
33, 46, 114, 210
Bush, George W.
initiates bailouts, 170,
212–213, 222, 242
–Paulson discussion on
collapsing economy,
195–213
political contributions,
122–123
preceded by roots of
collapse, 6
refuses to regulate Enron
energy trading, 130, 134
Treasury overpays in
purchases of toxic assets,
221

California energy crisis and
Enron
corrupt activity exposed,
127–130
deregulated energy market
effects, 127
price caps requested by
officials, 134–135

ricochet scheme, 130
rolling blackouts, consumers
bilked, 115, 124, 127, 134
Campaign contributions
by Arnall to G. W. Bush,
Republicans, 149
by Enron, Goldman, 8,
119–120, 122–123
by financial services industry,
62
by Ken Lay to candidates,
122
linked to international
projects, trade missions,
120–122
by lobbyists, 112
to Obama from private, Wall
Street, funds, 8, 239,
242–244
to Phil Gramm from Enron,
114, 124
by Wall Street, 7–8
Capitalism and government
restraint on corporate
actions, 18–19, 98
Carpenter, Michael A., 158
Causey, Richard A., 165
CDO liquidity put, 155
CDOs. *See* Collateralized debt
obligations
CDS. *See* Credit default swaps
Center for Economic and Policy
Research, 167
Center for Responsive Politics,
119, 122
CFMA. *See* Commodity Futures
Modernization Act

CFTC. *See* Commodity Futures
Trading Commission
Cheney, Richard "Dick," 134,
135
Chinese walls, 163, 166
Cho, David, 219
Citi Residential, 149
Citibank
merged with Travelers to
form Citigroup, 74
and Weill-Clinton phone
conversation, 58–59
Citicorp–Travelers Group
merger, 52, 53, 74, 76,
141–142
CitiFinancial, 76, 146
Citigroup
as creditor of Enron, 136
as heavy underwriter of
CDOs, 150
bailout deal created by
Geithner, Paulson, Rubin,
218–220
bailout expansion endorsed
by Obama, 218
in business with ACC Capital
Holdings, 147–149
buys predatory subprime
mortgage lenders, 76–78,
144–145, 148–149
conglomerate created,
141–142, 153
–Enron relations, 156–167
expands CDOs, risks, under
Rubin, 150, 154–156
formation forces Glass-
Steagall repeal, 52

influences New York Federal
Reserve, 218–220
regulatory inquiries, class
action lawsuits, 73–74
as too big to fail, 57
CitiMortgage, 76
Clinton, Hillary, 19–20, 70, 167
Clinton, William Jefferson "Bill"
allied with Republican
drafters of FSMA, 61
cancels government officials
lobbying restriction, 161
covered by Jesse Jackson's
FSMA endorsement, 68
on derivatives advice from
Rubin and Summers, 142
–Gramm compromise
weakens CRA, 65–66,
69–71, 77
–Greenspan agreement
defines economic policy,
99–100
and Rubinomics, 20
supports passage of CFMA,
106
triangulation political
strategy, 14, 65, 216–217
validates Citigroup merger,
legislation, 58–59
Clinton administration
boom benefits wealthiest
Americans, 15
economic policy defined,
99–100
ignores, condemns, Born's
derivatives warnings, 94,
101–102, 105

as instrumental in FSMA
   passage, 63–69
with Raines as Fannie Mae
   CEO, 185–186
role in deregulation, Glass-
   Steagall repeal, 6–7, 13,
   55–56
with roots of economic
   collapse, 6–7
trade missions linked to
   Enron, 120–121
Clinton bubble, 6, 188, 237
CLUES system, 180, 183
Collateralized debt obligations
   (CDOs)
   Citigroup as heavy
      underwriter, 143, 150, 154
   created by math models, 33
   described, 10, 33–34
   packaged as securities after
      deregulation, 71–72
Commercial Credit company,
   76
Committee to Save the World,
   81–82, 86, 140, 152
Commodity Futures
   Modernization Act
   (CFMA) of 2000
   bans regulations on
      derivatives, 37
   benefits Fannie
      Mae–Countrywide
      relations, 184
   blamed as cause of
      economic crisis by
      Obama, 108–109
   created by Phil Gramm, 32

Enron loophole measures
   written by Enron, 111,
   115, 117–118, 125–126
   passage, 79, 105–106
and Robertson conflict of
   interest, 123–124
Rubin's role in legislation,
   142, 157
stifles CFTC reform efforts,
   106
supported by Jesse Jackson,
   65–66
Commodity Futures Trading
   Commission (CFTC)
   chaired by Born (1996–1999),
      37, 91
   chaired by Goldman-alum
      Gensler, 224
   chaired by Wendy Gramm
      (1988–1993), 33–35,
      39–40, 114
   described, 83
   prohibited from studying,
      regulating, derivatives, 94,
      101–104, 106–107
Community Reinvestment Act
   (CRA)
   described, 62, 75–76
   weakened by Clinton–
      Gramm compromise,
      65–66, 69–71, 77
Competitive Equality Banking
   Act of 1987, 28–29
Computerized banking, 49
Computerized mathematical
   trading models, 37–38, 40,
   200–201

"Concept release" document
(Born), 41, 93–94, 102–104
Conflicts of interest between
public service and private
sector reward
for Geithner and Friedman,
234–237
for Goldman alumni,
201–202
for Paulson, 201–202
for Robertson, 115–116,
123–124
Rubin–Fisher phone call,
136–137, 158–161
Rubin's government-Citi-
Enron roles, 140–141,
156–167, 218–220
Summers hedge fund
payment, 230
Congress, U.S.
investigates AIG bonuses,
use of bailout money, 228
passes take-it-or-leave-it
bailout legislation,
205–206
passes CFMA, 96, 105–106
prohibits Born's derivatives
study, actions, 105
toughens financial industry
regulation (1987), 28–29
Congressional Black Caucus, 66,
68
Congressional Research Service,
126
Consumer and community
activists
on Citigroup's purchase of
Associates, 145

led by Jackson to weaken
CRA protections, 70
object to CFMA legislation,
66–67
and privacy protection, 61
Consumers Union, 145
Control Data Corporation, 76
Cooper Union speech (Obama),
17–19, 21–24
Cooper Union speech (Rubin),
20–21
Cornyn, John, 240
Countrywide
CLUES customer
creditworthiness
program, 180–181, 183
Friends of Angelo program,
179, 181
Mozilo-Johnson-Raines
arrangements, 176–185
strategic Fannie Mae
agreement, 182–185
sued by SEC for violations,
185
CRA. *See* Community
Reinvestment Act
Credit default swaps (CDS)
created by math models, 33
described, 9, 10, 108
with Goldman as AIG top
customer, 202, 228
lack of transparency, growth
rate, 200
risks dismissed by Wendy
Gramm, 36–37
Credit rating agencies
and Citigroup, 159–160
downgrade Enron, 136

and Enron-Dynegy merger,
    158, 164
rating system failure, 233
Creditworthiness evaluation. *See*
    CLUES system
Creswell, Julie, 201–202
Croatia/Bosnia trade mission,
    120

D. E. Shaw, 230
D'Amato, Alfonse, 64
Dash, Eric, 149, 152
Davis, Gray, 134
Davis, Lanny, 122
Debt, buying and selling, 8–10,
    20. *See also* Collateralized
    debt obligations
Democrats and Democratic Party
    blamed for banking,
        subprime, debacle, 71,
        75–76, 169
    concerned about weakening
        of CRA, 62, 65
    as guardians of FDR's mode
        of capitalism, 19
    surpass Republicans in
        campaign contributions
        from Wall Street
Deregulation of financial
    markets
    advocated by Carter, 31
    advocated by Clinton, 6–7,
        13, 30
    advocated by Reagan, 13,
        27–28, 30
    denounced by Obama in
        Cooper Union speech,
        21–24

enables creation of giant
    Citigroup, 141–142
government removed from
    authority by CFMA,
    106–107
leads to economic crisis,
    global recession, 3,
    162–163
Rubin pushes to create, 20,
    100, 142–143, 153, 223
Summers pushes to create,
    79, 94–95, 102–103, 154,
    230–232
Derivatives market
    described, 34
    Goldman packages with
        expectation of failure, 227
    not regulated, culminating in
        crash, 3, 40–41
    not understood by top
        executives, 200–201
    risks dismissed by Wendy
        Gramm, 35–36, 38
    self-regulation set forth by
        Greenspan, 97
    sliced into tranches by
        buyers of debts, 9, 38
    See also Bundled derivatives;
        Over-the-counter
        derivatives
Dimon, James L. "Jamie," 240,
    241
Dorgan, Byron, 57
Douglas, Jack, Jr., 120–121
Dynegy, 158, 163, 164–165

Earned Income Tax Credit
    (EITC), 217

Edgerton, Henry, 90
Energy trading
  California's rolling blackouts,
    115, 127–130
  Enron loophole allows
    manipulative practices,
    115, 126
  exempt from regulatory
    scrutiny, 115–116
  power plants taken offline by
    Enron, 127–130, 160
  price caps requested for
    California energy crisis,
    134–135
Enron
  –Citigroup close
    involvement, 156–167
  engages in accounting fraud,
    23
  implodes, collapses, 72, 74,
    116, 197
  links political donations to
    trade missions, 120–121
  lobbying leads to
    deregulation, meltdown,
    112–113, 117
  manipulates western U.S.
    energy, 115, 124, 127–130,
    134
  pressures Born against
    derivatives scrutiny, 85, 95
  and Wendy Gramm, 39, 56
  writes language into CFMA,
    117
Enron loophole, 115, 117–118,
  126
Equity stripping, 77

Falcon, Armando, Jr.
  attempts to regulate GSEs,
    172–174
  on Fannie Mae executives'
    greed, corruption,
    192–193
Fannie and Freddie. *See* Fannie
  Mae; Freddie Mac;
  Government sponsored
  enterprises
Fannie Mae
  Alternative Dream Initiative,
    178–179
  bailed out, nationalized, for
    $200 billion, 189–190, 197
  and Barney Frank, 171–172,
    180
  CEOs' compensation
    packages, 178, 187, 190
  invests in subprime, Alt-A,
    mortgages for profit, 174,
    179
  as quasi-government-
    sponsored, profit-driven,
    175–177, 187
  strategic agreement with
    Countrywide, 182–185
  uses Countrywide's
    customer evaluation
    program, 180, 183
Fastow, Andrew, 165
Federal Deposit Insurance
  Corporation (FDIC), 27,
  60
Federal Reserve Bank
  in jurisdiction rivalry with
    Treasury Department, 64

with Robertson as lobbyist,
115–116
rules against regulatory
barriers, 51
supports bailout of Long-
Term Capital
Management, 84
waives Citigroup compliance
with Glass-Steagall, 54–55
Federal Reserve Bank of New
York
and AIG bailout as backdoor,
204, 226–228, 235–237
–Citigroup relations, bailout
deal, 218–219, 223
Friedman's purchase of
Goldman stock, 234–235
and Geithner's role in bank
bailouts, 153–154, 204,
206–208
Finance, insurance, and real
estate firms. *See* FIRE
industries
Financial bubbles
amid complexity of
computer-driven models,
37–38
based on collatorized debt
due to deregulation, 14,
212
based on deregulated
derivatives, 126, 227, 230
housing, 188, 189, 227
See also Clinton bubble
Financial Crisis Inquiry
Commission, 173, 192
Financial market myths, 4–5

Financial markets
Obama proposes renewed
regulation, 108, 239–240
rapid changes in, 33
regulations strengthened by
Congress (1987), 28–29
See also Deregulation of
financial markets
Financial Services
Modernization Act
(FSMA) of 1999
enables creation of giant
Citigroup, 142
as Gramm-Leach-Bliley Act,
32, 62, 69
replaces Glass-Steagall Act, 55
tagged as Citigroup
Authorization Act, 71–72
FIRE industries, 26–27, 32
Fisher, Peter, 136–137, 158–160
Flipping, 77, 188
Frank, Barney, 171–172, 180
Fraud in the market
difficult to prove under
securities statues, 162
by Enron and Citigroup,
164–166
and Greenspan's notion of
self-regulating markets, 99
risked by hedge funds buying
toxic assets, 232–233
and swap exemption
language for Enron in
CFMA, 124–125
Freddie Mac
bailed out, nationalized, 197
compensation of CEOs, 187

Freddie Mac (*continued*)
  invests in subprime, Alt-A,
    mortgages for profit, 174
  as quasi-government-
    sponsored, profit-driven,
    175–177, 187
  shut out by Countrywide's
    relations to Fannie Mae,
    181–182
Free market
  and Fannie Mae, Freddie
    Mac, failures, 195, 197
  Greenspan's ideology, 99–100
  ideologues target GSEs,
    housing, 172, 197
  and need for regulation, 18
  and Obama on Dimon and
    Blankfein, 243
  propaganda of Reagan years,
    6
FSMA. *See* Financial Services
    Modernization Act of
    1999
Furman, Jason, 216, 218

Garn–St. Germain Depository
    Institutions Act, 13–14, 27
GE. *See* General
    Electric/General Electric
    Capital
Geithner, Timothy
  and backdoor bailout,
    236–237
  on failure of self-regulation,
    108–109
  and Lehman bankruptcy, 204
  as New York Fed chair,
    206–208, 218–220

in Obama administration,
    153, 220, 226
  role in AIG bailout
    benefiting Goldman,
    206–207, 226–227
General Accounting Office
  study of unregulated
    derivatives, 97
General Electric/General Electric
    Capital (GE), 25, 44–45
Gensler, Gary, 224–225
Gillespie, Ed, 119
Glass-Steagall Act of 1933
  described, 22, 27, 50
  economic crisis as
    consequence of repeal,
    23, 74, 75, 162
  and Obama economic plan,
    239, 241
  replaced by FSMA, 55–56,
    61–62
  restrictions extended by
    Congress (1987), 28–29
  reversal supported by FIRE
    firms, 32
Goldman Sachs
  alumni control government
    bailouts, 201–202, 223–224
  alumni used in Bush,
    Obama, administrations,
    201–202, 223–224, 226
  converts to holding
    company, qualifies for
    TARP, 196–197
  as Democratic Party
    contributor, 8
  gives CEO bonus of $68.7
    million, 244

as profitable beneficiary of
AIG bailout, 202–203,
211, 223, 227, 244
sells, packages, derivatives,
196, 227–228
Government sponsored
enterprises (GSEs)
bailed out by G. W. Bush
administration, 170–171
as private, profit-driven, 172,
175, 192–193
pursue subprime, Alt-A,
mortgages, 174, 191
Gramm, Phil
as antiregulatory, free-market
ideologue, 63, 216
background, 30–32
blames economic collapse on
victims, 56–57
responsible for CFMA, 32, 56
with ties to Enron, 114,
124–125
as UBS executive, 56, 216
weakens CRA standards for
poor consumers, 62,
68–71
Gramm, Wendy Lee
background, 25, 30
as deregulation activist, 33,
35–36
exempts Enron from
regulatory restraints, 114
as head of CFTC, 83, 131
under Reagan, targets
regulatory system, 26–27,
33–34
tries to unseat Bush's CFTC
commissioner, 130–133

Gramm-Latta budget of 1981,
30–31
Gramm-Leach-Bliley Act,
32–33, 62, 69
Grayson, Alan, 116, 189–191
Great Depression, 19, 22, 98,
187
Greenberger, Michael, 95, 96,
116–117
Greenspan, Alan
on bailout of Long-Term
Capital Management, 84
–Clinton agreement defines
economic policy, 99–100
declares free markets as self
regulating, 50
on growth of OTC
derivatives, 91
insists derivatives will self-
regulate, 97, 98
on irrational exuberance of
economy, 11
opposes Born's derivatives
study, stance, 94, 100,
101–102, 104–105
profiled, praised, in media,
86–88
in territorial rivalry with
Rubin, 64
GSEs. *See* Government
sponsored enterprises

Hedge funds
and AIG, 213
Geithner's reliance on
managers, 208
Long-Term Capital
Management, 84, 105

Hedge funds (*continued*)
  Paulson's description to G.
    W. Bush, 199
  receiving banks' toxic
    holdings, 229–230, 232
  regulations prevented by
    Summers, 230
Hendrickson, Jill M., 50–51
Hillebrand, Gail, 145
Hirsh, Michael, 107, 156
Housing
  affordability as original
    purpose of GSEs,
    174–175
  bubble denied by Raines, 188
  Fannie Mae, Freddie Mac,
    fail due to greed,
    corruption, 192–193
  flipped in hot market, 188
  and Goldman's toxic
    derivatives, 227–228
  not prime agenda of Fannie
    Mae, Freddie Mac, 187
Howard, J. Timothy, 190–191
Hurd, Maude, 77–78, 145–146

In an Uncertain World (Rubin), 94
India–Enron power plant
  project, 121–122
IndyMac Bank, 176
Insurance against bad loans. *See*
  Credit default swaps
Ip, Greg, 84, 117
Irwin, Neil, 219

Jackson, Jesse
  allied with funder Weill,
    67–68
  supports passage of CFMA,
    66
  supports weakening CRA
    protections, 69–70
  as trump card for Clinton's
    support, 65
Jefferson, Aisha, 191
Jeffery, Reuben, III, 202
Jester, Dan, 202
Johnson, James A.
  avoids accountability for
    crash, 185
  compensation at Fannie
    Mae, 185
  as Friend of Angelo Mozilo,
    179, 181
  profiled in media, 176–177
  teams with Countrywide's
    CLUES system, 180
J.P. Morgan/JP Morgan Chase
  acquires subprime lender
    Washington Mutual, 245
  bail out allowed, Geithner's
    role, 204, 208
  gives CEO bonus of $17
    million, 240
  invests in, tries to sell, Enron
    to Dynegy, 163, 164
  and Summers, 230

Kahn, Joseph, 160
Kantor, Mickey, 120–121
Kashkari, Neel T., 202
Kean, Steven J., 130
Kerry, John, 216
Kirkpatrick, David D., 240
Komansky, David, 63
Kraushaar, Judah S., 62–63

Krugman, Paul
  as critic of Garn–St.
    Germain . Act, 27
  on Reagan's culpability, 13
  on role of Fannie Mae and
    Freddie Mac, 172

LaBolt, Ben, 231
Langley, Monica, 58–59, 65,
  66–68
Lawsuit by University of
  California pension fund.
  See University of California
  pension fund lawsuit
Lay, Ken
  background, 113–114
  with Cheney, drafts G. W.
    Bush energy policy,
    134–135
  and Clinton, 120, 122
  contributes to political
    candidates, 119–120, 122
  expands Enron's contracts
    using loophole, 115
  as friend, donor, of G. W.
    Bush, 85, 123, 197
Leach, James, 65, 84, 85
Lehman Brothers
  allowed to fail, given rivalry
    with Goldman, AIG, 212,
    223
  Paulson's rationale for
    collapse, 204, 207
Leverage and risk
  with allowable debt increased
    for investment banks, 199
  at Citigroup, for sake of
    higher profits, 152

of consumers, 188
  as excessive, of financial
    institutions, 75, 96, 109,
    238
  government-financed, of
    Obama plan, 233
  Paulson on, 198
Levin, Mark R., 160
Levitt, Arthur
  admits underestimating
    derivatives danger, 96, 107
  on incomprehensibility of
    Greenspan, 97
  opposes Born's derivatives
    study, positions, 94,
    101–102, 104–105
Levy, Roger, 70
Lewan, Michael, 119
Lewis, Mark, 160
Liddy, Edward M., 203
Lieberman, Joe, 161
Liquidity as a problem
  and AIG, 211–212
  Bowsher's warning, 97–98
  Citigroup's CDO liquidity
    put, 155
  falsified by Enron, 165
Lobbying and lobbyists
  banking, 51
  Enron's corrupt process,
    112–113, 117–119
  expertise of, 111–112
  financial services industry
    campaign, 62
  limited in distributing TARP
    funds, 226
  with links to government
    officials, 114–116, 118, 122

Lobbying and lobbyists
  (*continued*)
  prevent regulation of GSEs,
    175
  thwart Obama financial
    reform attempts, 241
  write government rules, 176
Long, Chris, 124, 125–126
Long-Term Capital
  Management, 84, 85, 93,
    94, 96, 104–105
Low-income consumers and
  borrowers
  blamed for banking debacle
    by conservatives, 170
  and Clinton's economic
    policy, 216–217
  concerns over CFMA
    legislation, 66, 68–69
  CRA prevents mortgage
    redlining, 62
  against deregulation, 68
  and Fannie Mae–
    Countrywide CLUES
    program, 184–185
  and GSEs, 171
  as hard hit by banking
    meltdown, 178–179, 244
  and predatory subprime
    lending practices, 76–77,
    145–146, 188

Madoff, Bernard, 203
Markey, Edward J.
  as deregulation critic, 97–98,
    116
  as privacy advocate, 61

McCain, John
  embraces Wall Street
    philosophy, 215
  Phil Gramm's campaign
    involvement, 56, 63, 216
McDonough, Bill, 94
McLarty, Thomas "Mack,"
    121–122
McMahon, Jeffrey, 165
Media (business)
  covers Johnson's Fannie Mae
    mortgage derivatives
    spree, 185
  defers to Greenspan's self-
    regulation position, 98
  exposes Rubin-government-
    Citigroup-Enron conflicts,
    152–167
  extols Greenspan, Rubin,
    Summers, 86–88, 140,
    152, 161
  fails to question Clinton
    policies, 15
  misses, ignores, signs leading
    to crash, 2–3
  Rubin-Fisher phone call
    coverage, 158–161
  supports merger formation
    of Citigroup, 54–55
Mercatus Center, George
    Mason University, 26, 39
Middle class investors and
  borrowers
  Reich suggests unreturnability
    of prosperity, 17
  scapegoated for economic
    crash, 11, 170

in stock market, e-trade, growth, bubble, 10–11, 44
support Clinton, 7
Modernization, as term, 55, 60, 67
Moody's credit rating agency, 158, 160, 164
Mooney, Brian C., 147
Morgan Stanley, 207, 208, 211
Morgenson, Gretchen, 180–181, 189–190, 207–208, 219
Mortgage loans
   African Americans as hardest hit group in meltdown, 244
   bundled, sold, as CDOs, 10
   See also Collateralized debt obligations; Subprime mortgage lending
Mozilo, Angelo
   close relations with Johnson, Raines, Fannie Mae, 176, 179, 180–182
   on Fannie Mae–Countrywide strategic agreement, 184
   sued by SEC for violations, 185
Muolo, Paul, 181–182

Nader, Ralph, 60, 68
National Economic Council (NEC), 218
National Women's Law Center, 90
New Century Financial Corporation, 144

New Deal regulations of the market economy, 6–7, 18–19, 23
New York Federal Reserve Bank. *See* Federal Reserve Bank of New York
Newsome, James E., 130–133
Nichols, John, 135
No Banker Left Behind program, 228
Nonrecourse loans, 233

Obama, Barack
   campaign funding from private, Wall Street, sources, 8, 239, 242–244
   with Geithner as Treasury secretary, 153, 218
   pre-election economic analysis, critique, 17–20, 21–24
   with Summers in administration, 153, 218, 229, 231
   uses Rubin, Rubin's economic team, 153, 167, 216, 218, 220
Obama economic program
   allows collusion between buyers, sellers, of assets, 233
   banks' toxic holdings turned over to hedge funds, 229, 232
   condemns CFMA (June 2009), 108

Obama economic program
    (*continued*)
  endorses Citigroup bailout,
      218
  expands AIG bailouts,
      222–223
  health care legislation diverts
      attention, 242
  influenced by antiregulatory
      Goldman alumna,
      223–224, 226
  mortgage foreclosure
      prevention ineffective, 245
  promises supervision of
      derivatives dealers, 238
  proposes renewed
      regulations, reform, 4,
      108, 239–240
  reacts to Mass. voters upset
      (January 2010), 239
  stops short of regulation,
      scrutiny, of markets, 4,
      245–246
  supports Wall Street, not
      homeowners, 220–221
O'Donnell, Thomas, 185
On the Brink (Paulson), 195–211
Over-the-counter derivatives
    (OTC)
  Born focuses on needed
      oversight, regulation, 84,
      92–93
  CFTC prohibited from
      studies, 94, 101–102
  described as driving U.S.
      prosperity, 103–104, 225

  explained, 7, 8–9
  notional value growth, 36–37

Pacific Gas & Electric Company,
    134
Palin, Sarah, 195, 209, 241, 243
Palmer, Mark, 123
Parsons, Richard, 144
Partnoy, Frank, 101
Patrick, Deval, 147, 148–149
Patterson, Mark, 226
Paulson, Henry M. Jr.
  admits financial sector's
      responsibility for collapse,
      1, 199
  bails out, receives blank
      check for, Citigroup, 213,
      219–220
  briefs G. W. Bush on
      collapsing economy,
      195–213
  criticized for Lehman
      downfall, 204, 207
  designs, puts through,
      AIG–Goldman bailouts,
      210–211, 223, 228
  directs Obama, McCain, on
      campaign content, 209
  downplays subprime
      mortgage dangers, 205
  issues $700 billion bailout
      proposal to Congress,
      205–206
Pearlstein, Steven, 220
Pecora, Ferdinand, 50
Perlowitz, Jeffrey, 149–150

Piketty, Thomas, 14–15
Presidential Economic
    Recovery Advisory
    Board, 241
President's Working Group on
    Financial Markets, 94–95,
    102
Price caps on wholesale energy
    sales, 130, 134–135
Prince, Charles O. III, 150–152,
    154–155
Public Citizen, 114, 119, 127

Quinn, Jack, 119

Raines, Franklin Delano
    avoids accountability for
        crash, 185
    compensation at Fannie
        Mae, 178, 187, 193
    manipulates books, earnings,
        targets, bonuses, 190–193
    relations with Countrywide's
        Mozilo, 179
Raisler, Ken, 95
Ramo, Joshua Cooper, 86–87
Rand, Ayn, 99, 101
Reagan, Ronald
    as advocate for unregulated
        market, 13, 27–29, 30
    appoints corporate-
        sympathetic government
        monitors, 33
    signs Garn–St. Germain
        Depository Institutions
        Act, 13, 27

and Wendy Gramm's key
    role, 25–26, 33
Reagan Revolution, 25, 46
The Real Deal (Weill and
    Kraushaar), 62–63, 68–69
Recession
    as deep, lasting, 16–17
    denied, blamed on victims,
        by Phil Gramm, 56–57
    global, 2–3, 10
    Rubin's perfect storm
        rationalization, 156
Reed, John S., 52, 58–60
Reed, Ralph, 119
Reich, Robert, 16 17, 100
Republicans and Republican
    Party
    with Arnall as major donor,
        149
    conservatives blame the poor
        for crash, 170
    cut taxes for richest brackets,
        15
    deregulation stance
        embraced by Clinton, 105
    with Enron as major donor,
        85, 119
    pressure Obama's proposed
        reforms, 239–241
Risk management
    dismissed by Wendy
        Gramm, 33, 38
    mathematical models, 9, 33
Robertson, Linda
    as Enron lobbyist, 115, 123,
        135–136

Robertson, Linda (*continued*)
    as Federal Reserve lobbyist,
        115–116, 133
    serves under Treasury
        secretaries, 115, 118, 123,
        137
Robinson, Walter V., 120
Roosevelt, Franklin Delano, 18,
    43, 55
Rubin, Robert E., in Clinton
    administration
    engineers Wall Street-first
        economic policy, 100
    opposes Born's derivatives
        study, positions, 94,
        100–105
    profiled, praised, in media,
        86–88, 140, 161
    pushes to create deregulation
        legislation, 20, 142–143,
        153
    relates to Weill, 63
    rivalry with Greenspan, 64
Rubin, Robert E., with Citigroup
    conflicts of interest
        discussed, 3, 79, 140–143
    dismisses crash as noncrisis,
        cycle, 20–21
    on economic perfect storm,
        2–3, 156
    involved with Enron,
        156–167 (*see also*
        Rubin-Fisher phone call)
    role in Citigroup downfall,
        disavowals, 146, 152–158,
        219–220

Rubin-Fisher phone call,
    136–137, 158–161
Rubinomics, 2, 20

Saez, Emmanuel, 14–15
Safire, William, 60–61
Salomon Smith Barney, 185
Sanders, Bernie, 224
Schroeder, Michael, 84, 104,
    117
Schwartz, Nelson D., 152
Securities and Exchange
    Commission (SEC)
    increases allowable debt for
        investment banks, 179
    investigates, sues,
        Countrywide, 181, 185
    limited by CFMA from
        regulating OTC
        derivatives, 108
    on Wendy Gramm, 133
Self-regulation of financial
    markets
    assumption enables ruin, 43
    declared by Greenspan, 50,
        97, 98
    limitations, 155
    Reagan's expectations, 46
    ultimately rejected by
        Geithner, Summers, 109
    as Wendy Gramm's
        argument, 39, 40
Shafran, Steve, 202
Shelby, Richard, 61
Sherman, Brad, 205
Skilling, Jeff, 125, 165

Snohomish County Public Utility District, Washington, 127–130

Spencer, Leanne, 190–191

Sperling, Gene, 63, 65, 69

Spirit of Glass-Steagall, 239, 241

Stanley, Allesandra, 160

Stevenson, Richard, 179

Stiglitz, Joseph E., 74–75, 79

Stimulus package, 222

Subprime mortgage lending
with Citigroup as top underwriter, 143–145, 146, 149
crisis harms African American households, 244–245
described, 35
by Fannie Mae and Freddie Mac, 174
grows, protected, after CFMA passage, 71, 106
with racially, economically, bifurcated patterns, 77–78

Summers, Lawrence
accuses Born of destabilizing financial markets, 95, 102–105
as antiregulatory, 74, 79, 100, 104
benefits from unregulated hedge funds, 229–230
calls for derivatives regulation under Obama, 104, 108–109
in Clinton administration, 64
declares deregulation secure, driving prosperity, 102–103, 231–232
on economic crash, 16
enables Enron to avoid scrutiny, 124–125
in Obama administration, 218, 229
paid by Lehman, Goldman, Citigroup, JPMorgan Chase, 229–231
profiled, praised, in media, 86–88

Supreme Court ruling on campaign finance, 246

Swaps. *See* Credit default swaps

Tapper, Jake, 142

TARP funds, 143, 196, 226, 232

Tea Party, 241, 243

Tearing Down the Walls (Langley), 58–59

Telecommunications sector deregulation, 23, 97, 176

Thomas, Evan, 156

Too big to fail conglomerates
AIG, 5, 210, 212
Citigroup, 5, 57, 142, 212
Safire's warning, 60

Toxic assets
bought back in bailouts, 220–221
of Citigroup guaranteed by government, 57, 142–143
of Lehman, 210
and nonrecourse loans, 233

Transparency
  in banking ends during
    Clinton years, 220
  in Born's concept document,
    93
  increased by regulations, 35
  lacking in CDS, 200
  needed in OTC derivatives
    trading, 82
Travelers Group, 52, 53, 74, 76,
  142
Treasury Department
  asked by Rubin to intervene
    for Enron, 136–137
  Geithner as secretary (2009),
    220, 226
  with Goldman alumni
    presence, 202
  inspector general's report,
    232–233, 236
  offers swap exemption
    language in CFMA,
    124–125
  officials linked to Enron, 115
  Paulson as secretary
    (2006–2009), 201
  Rubin as secretary
    (1995–1999), 12, 79
  Summers as secretary
    (1999–2001), 12, 79
Tull, John E. Jr., 95

UBS, 56, 216, 241
University of California pension
  fund lawsuit, 59, 162,
  164–166

Velie, Franklin B., 162
Volcker, Paul, 239–240, 241

Wall Street Project, 67
Wal-Mart, 216–217
Washington Mutual, 245
Waxman, Henry, 135
Weill, Sanford
  creates Citigroup, endorsed
    by Clinton, 52, 55–59, 154
  and FSMA passage, 62–71
  on Geithner, 218–219
Weisberg, Jacob, 136
Weisskopf, Michael, 121–122
Whalley, Greg, 136
White, Ben, 201–202
Williams, Bill III, 128–129
Wolf, Robert, 241
Women's Legal Defense Fund,
  90
WorldCom, 23, 72, 74

Yip, Pamela, 145

Zacchino, Narda, 88–89